CW00554710

To
Dave,

with best wishes

Fire-step to Fokker Fodder

Christmas 2021

FIRE-STEP TO FOKKER FODDER

FROM THE TRENCHES TO THE RED BARON
THE FIRST WORLD WAR DIARIES OF
WILLIAM 'JACK' LIDSEY

ANDREW WHITE

Published in 2019 by Fighting High Ltd,
www.fightinghigh.com

Copyright © Fighting High Ltd, 2019
Copyright text © Andrew White, 2019

British Library Cataloguing-in-Publication data.
A CIP record for this title is available from the
British Library.

ISBN – 13: 978-1-9998128-7-4

Designed and typeset in Adobe Minion 11/15pt
by Michael Lindley. www.truthstudio.co.uk.

Printed and bound by Gomer Press.
Front cover design by www.truthstudio.co.uk.

For all those Old Brackleians who gave everything;
Sicut Lilium

Contents

Lieutenant General Jonathon Riley,
CB, DSO, PhD, MA, FRHists

Jack Lidsey was in very many ways a typical example of the best sort of young officer produced by the British Army during the First World War, and very much a child of his age and time. He was educated at an English grammar and boarding school, Magdalen College, Brackley, and had enlisted less than a month after the outbreak of war as a volunteer in the newly formed (in 1908) Territorial Force, joining the 4th Battalion of the Oxford & Buckinghamshire Light Infantry as a private. Volunteers in the Territorial Force (TF) had no obligation to serve overseas in times of emergency unless they volunteered to do so – and Jack of course did. After war was declared in August 1914 the TF began rapidly to expand, by dividing battalions and filling up the spaces with new recruits, and Jack found himself in the 1/4th Battalion of his regiment. With this battalion, after mobilisation and training, he went to France in the dark days of March 1915 where it joined the 48th (South Midland) Division.

Jack served as a private soldier on tours of trenches in sectors around Ypres in Belgium and the Somme. This experience of being a private soldier will never have left him, and would have formed much of his later view of military life, for as one at the bottom of the military food chain, he would have known very well what styles of leadership worked and which did not; how the led responded to their leaders – good and bad; and how important were basic administration, hot food, good billets, courage and example, and simple compassion.

By early 1916 the British Army had expanded from its original seven regular and nine TF divisions to more than fifty divisions in France and

Flanders alone. With such an expansion came an urgent need for officers. Having been to a suitable school, Jack was a prime candidate and in February of that year he was sent to an officer cadet battalion. From there he returned to 1/4th Ox & Bucks to command a platoon of between thirty and forty men. Having been a private soldier for almost two years and seen active service, he would have had none of the problems of inexperience and uncertainty faced by so many pink-cheeked young gentlemen joining a seasoned unit in the line. Jack would know all the old soldiers' tricks!

Jack arrived in May, just in time for the great Somme Offensive, which began on 1 July. Here, he and his platoon came under the command of Lieutenant General Sir Aylmer Hunter-Weston, 'Hunter-Bunter', the general officer commanding VIII Corps and one of the stupidest and most ineffective of the First World War generals: a fine example of the type that gave every general a bad name. The Ox & Bucks were lucky to escape the carnage of 1 July in their sector around Serre as they were held in reserve. However, they were subsequently called on to support the Australians in the assault on Pozières, where they suffered badly. Jack fortunately was unhurt. His diaries for this period are similar to those of many other literate, informed young men – but given his breadth of experience and his education they are extraordinarily vivid and a wonderful addition to the narrative of the infantry in the First World War. His glimpses of the small changes of daily life in the trenches illuminate a war that is beyond the ability of almost all of us today to understand or even imagine.

The real interest of this book, however, lies in the period from November 1916 to March 1917 when he transferred into the Royal Flying Corps. His diaries give no indication as to why he made the move – perhaps he had simply had enough of the squalor of trenches and the near-inevitability of death or a wound. Without any sort of formal training, Jack joined No. 16 Squadron at Bruay, near Arras, equipped with the notoriously slow, underpowered and poorly armed BE2, a two-seater plane used chiefly for directing artillery fire. In this aircraft he served as an observer and again his diary gives a terrific insight into the daily life, the frustrations, the excitement and the fears of the early days of aerial combat in what was essentially a large and flimsy kite powered by a lawn-mower engine.

No. 16 Squadron was assigned to the Canadian Corps for the build-up to the Nivelle Offensive in April 1917, and during this period Lidsey and his pilot, Sid Quicke, were involved in several air-to-air combats, and on at least one occasion they faced the dreaded 'Red Baron', Manfred von Richthofen, but escaped and lived to tell the tale. However, on 21 March 1917, the Red Baron proved too much of an adversary. Jack and Sid were shot down; Quicke was killed at once but Jack survived in hospital until the following day. His original wooden grave cross hangs on the chapel wall at Magdalen College School, where the author told me that 'I used to wonder about it when I was an inattentive schoolboy in Chapel.'

Andrew White is well qualified to have written this excellent book, having himself served in the Royal Air Force on active service and having been acquainted with Jack Lidsey's story for many years. I am honoured to have been asked to introduce this book, which fascinated me from the moment I picked it up, and congratulate Andrew on having put together such a valuable addition to the literature of the life of the fighting man in the First World War.

Llanllwni, Carmarthenshire
August 2018

Preface

I was born and raised in the market town of Brackley, which nestles in the Ouse Valley at the southern tip of the county of Northamptonshire. Northants is a county that, to me, never seems to know quite where it belongs. Long, narrow, and laying diagonally across the heart of the country, some might place it in East Anglia; others in the East Midlands; and others still in the South East. This confusion was evident in our family home via the regional news channels that we received on the television: downstairs in the living room, we watched the London news on the BBC, but the Midlands news over on ITV; meanwhile, on my portable set upstairs, we could tune in to Anglia TV. So, we could cover the day's events from Southwark to Solihull, and Lowestoft to Leicester.

This sense of not belonging anywhere definite knocked on to Brackley itself. The town lies right on the borders with neighbouring Oxfordshire and Buckinghamshire, and has more in common with the Home Counties than, say, the steel town of Corby in the north of the County. Brackley had once been at the hub of two railways, the London North Western and the Great Central, but Beeching's cuts in the 1960s closed both the town's lines and its two stations, leaving it largely isolated save for its location mid-way between Oxford and Northampton on the main A43 trunk road, but the building of the town's bypass in the 1980s further added to its seclusion. When asked where I am from, I usually add 'near Silverstone', to give a more familiar location to the enquirer.

There is history to the town, however, dating back to the Romans. Placed at the crossroads of the trade routes from London to Birmingham and Oxford to Cambridge, Brackley was a prosperous wool trading centre in the Middle Ages, boasting a castle and two hospitals. In 1215, the barons plotting against King John used the town as their base from which to negotiate with the King, who was at Oxford. Shuttle diplomacy commenced, but John ultimately rejected the rebels' terms, so they promptly renounced their oaths of allegiance to the Crown and declared civil war. The demands set out by the barons, known as the 'Brackley Schedules', formed the basis of Magna Carta, sealed by King John later at Runnymede. Less dramatically, Brackley was the unnamed 'market town' in Flora Thompson's *Lark Rise to Candleford* trilogy of books, set among the outlying villages. These highlights aside, there is not much else remarkable about Brackley, summarised by Pigot & Co's Directory of 1831 as possessing 'but little to recommend it to the observation of the tourist'.

It was into this somewhat anonymous town that I arrived in 1964, a place that was to be the centre of my universe for the next twenty-one years until I joined the Royal Air Force. I was born in Brackley Cottage Hospital; my father (and grandfather before him) ran a butcher's shop in the town. My education took place there, from infants to 'A' Levels, and my leisure and relationships were all conducted within the town's small boundaries. Since I left in the mid-1980s, those boundaries have sprawled; the construction close by of the M40, the imminent arrival of HS2, and the associated influx of light industry have seen growth, the scale of which has almost absorbed some of the closer villages that I used to cycle to in my youth.

My secondary education took place at Magdalen College School, Brackley. The school has a rich and fascinating history covering almost 500 years, and still retains links with its founding establishment, Magdalen College, Oxford. The seeds for this book were sown when, as a daydreaming pupil sitting in the school chapel for a service one afternoon, I noticed four simple wooden crosses suspended on one wall. The crosses were those of former pupils killed during the First World War and had presumably marked their final resting places until more permanent headstones could be erected. My attention was brought sharply back to the sermon after a stern word from one of the teachers, and I thought little more about the crosses.

Until the 1990s, that is. By then, I was a junior officer in the RAF with more than a passing interest in military history. Standing in one of the myriad of Commonwealth War Graves Commission cemeteries that dot the Somme region one wet day, I recalled the grave markers back at Magdalen Chapel. I found myself wondering if the crosses were still there, and who those boys were that they commemorated; had anyone ever researched their stories? A visit to the chapel shortly afterwards confirmed that the crosses were indeed still on the wall. I jotted down the scant information (not much more than name, rank and number) etched on to them, and decided to see what I could find out. My original intent was only to satisfy my own curiosity by putting a little more detail to the names, but after several years of non-constant research, one story stood out among them, that of William John Lidsey. He, like me, was a Magdalen boy.

British Army Infantry Organisation, 1914 – 1918

Army: Consisting of two or more corps, between 100,000 to 250,000 men; commanded by a general.

Corps: Consisting of two to five divisions, between 50,000 to 125,000 men; commanded by a lieutenant general.

Division: Consisting of three brigades; between 16,000 to 18,000 men; commanded by a major general.

Brigade: Consisting of three battalions, approximately 4,000 men; commanded by a brigadier general.

Battalion: Consisting of four companies (plus one HQ company), approximately 1,000 men; commanded by a lieutenant colonel.

Company: Consisting of four platoons, approximately 200 men; commanded by a major or senior captain.

Platoon: Consisting of four sections, between 30 to 40 men; commanded by a lieutenant or second lieutenant.

Section: Between 7 to 10 men; commanded by a corporal.

Royal Flying Corps Organisation, 1914 – 1918

Brigade: Consisting of two wings; commanded by a brigadier general.

Wing: Consisting of up to nine squadrons (by 1918), but more usually four or five; commanded by a lieutenant colonel.

Squadron: Consisting of three flights, approximately 12 aircraft in total; commanded by a major.

Flight: Consisting of 6 to 10 pilots (and a corresponding number of observers); commanded by a captain.

All the above are approximate figures, varying with a number of factors.

Introduction

Keeping a diary or journal during the First World War (or indeed any war) was by no means unusual for soldiers. A notebook could be a place of refuge from the trauma of the conflict, somewhere to confide thoughts, hopes, doubts and fears at a time when such things would almost certainly have gone unsaid between the men in the front line. Perhaps, too, those written words would later have served to help the writer remember, reflect, and come to terms with what he had been through once the fighting was over. As a private record between the compiler and the mute confidant of the diary, there was no intention to have the papers published, but, with the passing of the First World War generation, several such wartime accounts have now been printed, giving us an insight into the lives of those who left behind the world they knew for one which they never could have imagined. Today, things are very different, as people are willing – and seem to need – to share their innermost views and emotions instantly with a wide, even global, audience through social media. With Facebook, Twitter feeds and Instagram, hardly anything is kept secret any more.

Jack Lidsey was by no means an extraordinary young man. He came from a farming background in 'Middle England', and was the product of a local grammar school. What is different about him, and therefore what makes his diaries stand out from others, is the path that his wartime career followed. He was one of the first to volunteer, in the first month of the war, and went overseas as a private soldier – the lowest of the low. He was promoted early on, and was then selected for commissioning as an officer, becoming one of the very first products of the new officer cadet battalions. Lidsey rejoined his regiment as a subaltern just in time for the Battle of the Somme, where, as we shall see, he fought hard and was extremely fortunate to survive. With that particular confrontation over, Jack volunteered for the Royal Flying Corps, an occupation just as dangerous, if not more so, than anything he had endured thus far as a soldier in the trenches. As an untrained observer in an aeroplane with a particularly undesirable reputation, he flew and fought in the skies over the Western Front, where, ultimately, he met his end at the hands of the most successful fighter pilot of the First World War.

Lidsey made a diary entry almost every day for the two years of his war, from landing in France in March 1915, to the day before he was killed in March 1917. Through his writings, we learn how life developed for the citizen soldier, and follow the progression of the First World War from its early months to just past its mid-point. Most importantly, he gives us a rare view of the lot of an aviator during the worst period of attrition in the air of the entire war.

I first learned of Lidsey's diaries some years ago and attempted to get sight of them through a private collector, but without success. Later, I discovered that copies were held by the Imperial War Museum in London and also the RAF Museum at Hendon, but I wanted to approach his family to see if they had the originals, and to ask their permission to write his story based on them. It took a great deal of detective work to finally track down Emma, his great-niece, but once I had explained to her what I wanted to do, she gained the family's agreement and sent me a transcript of the diaries (the originals are pencil-written in four pocket notebooks and are too precious to be handled), as well as photographs and other documents. The transcript has an introductory page written by Lidsey's younger brother Richard, himself a First World War veteran who was Mentioned in Despatches, and I reproduce some of his words here, as they sum up the diaries perfectly: 'A simple unadorned account of the daily life experienced by the British "civilian soldier" in the 1914/18 war. Obviously written with no thought of publication, there is neither exaggeration nor dramatisation, nor any attempt to create "a story". There is an absence of the "horror element", as those of us who experienced war at the "sharp end" well know, that was too horrible to be recorded in writing. I think that it is valuable for future generations in showing the truly appalling physical conditions which were endured by ordinary human beings for months and years on end without a breakdown of morale.'

I would argue, though, that while Lidsey does mostly avoid graphic detail about the carnage he witnessed, there is more than enough in what he writes, and the way he writes it, to bring the 'horror element', as his brother puts it, home to the reader. What follows, then, is the experience of just one of the hundreds of thousands of casualties of the First World War.

Chapter One

Banbury and Brackley, 1895 – 1914

The date of 6 June 1895 was a very special day in the young lives of William Isaac Richard Lidsey and his wife, Emily. They had only been married the year before, but on that day, 24-year-old Emily delivered the couple's first child, a son. In keeping with the tradition of the times, they decided to name him after his father and grandfather, however the new-born William John Lidsey would henceforth always be known as John, or less formally, Jack. William and Emily would go on to have two more sons, Richard Stephen, two years after Jack, and Arthur James in 1901.

Jack's father was, like his grandfather, a tenant farmer in the village of Middle Littleton near Evesham.[1] The principal landowner in the village was Lord Northwick, who had been the local MP before inheriting the baronetcy and entering the House of Lords, so it seems likely that William rented the land from him. William later moved some ten miles to the south-east, to the village of Lower Lemington, near Moreton-in-Marsh, where he was again a tenant farmer. The land here was mainly meadow and pasture, with only a small amount given over to arable, and virtually everyone in the tiny community was employed on one of the three farms in the village.[2] In the Lidseys' case, the term 'tenant farmer' is slightly misleading; Jack's grandfather, for example, farmed 450 acres and employed ten men and four boys to help him do so, despite not owning the land.[3]

It was at Lower Lemington that William and Emily began their family. When it came time to send their eldest boy off to his first school, they chose a private primary school, Wisteria House, in Shipston-on-Stour, a little over four miles away.[4] Wisteria House School was run by two spinsters, Miss Ryder and Miss Legge, and had a reputation locally as a school for 'young gentlemen', and certainly not an establishment for the likes of the ordinary boys of the village.

William senior was clearly a successful and prosperous farmer as, aside from sending his son (and later his middle son, Richard) to a private school, he bought an estate called Hardwick Farm on the northern edge of Banbury, in Oxfordshire, when Jack was ten years old. The Hardwick estate was an ancient one, having been part of the Bishop of Lincoln's property in the Middle Ages, and modern archaeological surveys also show Roman features on the site.[5] In 1224 the Bishop of Lincoln granted to one William of Hardwick, for life, '1½ yardland in Bourton and a house in Hardwick'. The overlordship of Hardwick was held by the bishops of Lincoln until sold in 1547 to the Duke of Somerset. In 1548 Somerset sold the overlordship to Sir Anthony Cope, a colourful character who was MP for Banbury and later the High Sheriff of Oxfordshire, and who was gaoled in the Tower of London in 1587 for presenting the Speaker of the House of Commons with a Puritan revision of the Book of Common Prayer and a bill abrogating existing ecclesiastical law. Hardwick Farm remained in the hands of various members of the Cope family until 1727 when it was mortgaged to the Jenkinson family, before being sold to Samuel Gist, a hugely wealthy land (particularly in the United States) and slave owner, in 1800. William Lidsey bought the land from the trustees and executors of the estate of another, later, Samuel Gist, a descendant of the original, who had died in 1905 and was apparently of 'unsound mind'.[6] The Gists lived near William, at the family seat of Wormington Grange in Gloucestershire, so he perhaps knew the family and therefore had early knowledge of the availability of Hardwick.

The farm estate included a large house called Hardwick Farmhouse (later known as Hardwick House), which dated from the sixteenth century and was reputed to have incorporated various features, including windows and doorways, from Cope's original manor house that had been situated a short distance to the north of the building.[7] It was to this house that William moved his growing family, and from where Jack and his younger brothers would spend their formative years.

William Lidsey saw the Hardwick estate as an investment, believing that the growth of Banbury would push up prices as the demand for land rose. Evidently a shrewd businessman, he was later to be proved right when, in 1929, he sold sixteen hectares of the farm to a Canadian mining and aluminium production firm, the Northern Aluminium Company (NAC). The sale contract was signed after some delay on 15 February 1930; it appears that NAC refused to pay the asking price of £12,000 (equivalent to around £750,000 in 2018) demanded by William, offering only £10,000. The difference was met by the Gillett banking family of Banbury and by contributions from the aldermen of the town council who saw the value of attracting such a large company to Banbury.[8] Such was the growth of NAC, later better known as Alcan, that by the early 1950s the Banbury economy had largely become dependent on the prosperity of the aluminium rolling mill and laboratory that NAC built on the Hardwick site in 1931.

A few years after moving into Hardwick House, Jack's parents turned their attention to his secondary education. Despite being able to afford to buy Hardwick, or possibly because of it, they decided not to have him educated privately, but to send him instead to a grammar school. Since Banbury did not have such a school at the time (Banbury boys generally either went to 'a commercial school in the town or to middle school in Bloxham'[9]), the nearest option was Magdalen College School in the market town of Brackley, some ten miles away. The school was a small one, with fewer than 100 pupils, but such was its reputation that it took in boys from as far afield as Lancashire and Kent as boarders, as well as day-boys from the Brackley area. The local landowner, the Earl of Ellesmere, was a patron, and he awarded a gold medal annually to the boy who topped the summer examinations.[10] Young Jack Lidsey entered the school in January 1908, aged twelve, and joined his class-mates of Form I.[11] Given the distance from Hardwick House to Brackley, he was a boarder at Magdalen, as were his two brothers later, and all three were at the school together by 1911.[12] It may be that they boarded weekly, going home at the weekends on the train from Brackley Town station on the London & North Western line into Banbury.

Magdalen College School, Brackley, was one of three 'ancient' schools that fell under the wing of its Oxford University college namesake, the others being located in Oxford itself, and at Wainfleet in Lincolnshire.

The Brackley school was originally the Hospital of St James and St John, founded around 1150 by Robert le Bossu, Earl of Leicester. In 1484 the hospital was purchased by William Waynflete, Bishop of Winchester, as a place of refuge for Magdalen College, Oxford, to allow its students to escape the city during times of plague.[13] Therefore, the earliest lessons were perhaps delivered on the site as early as 1485, although no records to prove this exist, and in any case, it was probably a short-lived period, after which a chantry occupied the buildings. The most likely date for the formal foundation of the school is 1548 when further migrations of students from Oxford took place.[14] Later in the sixteenth century the school fell into disrepair, before renovation at the time of the Civil War. The refurbishment of the main school buildings apparently did not extend to the chapel and, despite being one of the largest and oldest school chapels in the country, its roof was stripped of lead in 1669 and the building fell into ruin. A pattern of repair and disuse for the chapel repeated itself over the next two hundred years, but since the last major restoration in 1870, the school chapel has been in regular use by both the students and the local community, and even today former pupils are able to be married in it.

Like most grammar and public schools, sport played a major part in the life of Magdalen, Brackley. Football was the winter game (phased out by rugby in 1925)[15], with cricket during the summer term. Matches of both were played against other schools and local men's teams, with school colours awarded for representation. The school also boasted an out-door swimming pool, and athletics were held in the Easter term. Jack Lidsey proved to be an all-round sportsman while at Magdalen and gained his colours in both football and cricket. His pen-picture in the school magazine, *The Brackleian*, for the 1912 season cricket XI remarks that 'he has come on a great deal since the beginning of the season; is still inclined to hit with a cross bat; is a good field and has made several smart catches'. As a middle-order batsman, his figures for that year made for dismal reading though – in sixteen innings, he made just thirty runs, with a highest score of six.[16] Averaging a lowly two and a half runs per innings (taking his four 'not outs' into account), Lidsey barely troubled the scorers, although he did take eight catches during that summer.

He was a far better footballer, although he did not start out as one of the star players, when participating on the left side of midfield, as his team biography in the 1911 Christmas term edition of *The Brackleian* makes plain: 'W J Lidsey – Outside-left: a very erratic player who is in too much of a hurry to get rid of the ball; should remember that one centre placed gently in front of goal is worth any number kicked wildly behind; might with advantage learn to trap the ball and to draw his man before passing.'[17] A report in the magazine on a match against the Church Institute team on 11 November 1911, made the point bluntly: 'W J Lidsey at outside left was weak, kicking much too wildly.'[18] The following year Jack changed position to centre forward where he was far more successful, becoming the team's vice-captain and a regular goal scorer for the school. His 1912 school football XI profile in *The Brackleian* records the significant development he had made in his game: 'W J Lidsey – Vice-Captain, Centre forward – Has greatly improved this season. His pace has been a great help in the forward line, though his shooting was painfully erratic; should learn to trap the ball. He was a most capable substitute for the captain during his indisposition in the Easter term.' Match reports in the magazine were also somewhat more complimentary than the previous year; in a game against Aylesbury Grammar School on 14 December 1912, which Magdalen won 4–2, for instance: 'In the second half we had by far the best of the game and scored twice more, the first goal coming from W J Lidsey who raced the Aylesbury backs and scored with a good low shot ... W J Lidsey played very well for the School and got the forwards together more often than in any previous match.'[19]

    As well as team sports, Jack did well in athletics. He was a sprinter and hurdler, competing in school sports days from 1910 to 1913, and was placed every year. He came second in the 100 yards in 1912, losing to a boy named P.S. Timms[20] (winning time – 11 seconds) by half a yard after 'an exciting finish'. Lidsey was to have his revenge the following year, winning the same event in a time of 12 seconds. He also came second in the 1912 hurdles, pipped by Timms again who won by three yards; 'unfortunately the stop-watch collapsed at this point and a good time was not recorded'[21].

    Due no doubt to his sporting prowess, by the Michaelmas term of 1912 Lidsey had become the captain of Lovel House, one of the school's three houses, a trusted and auspicious position. That year, he was also prominent in the Debating Society, opposing such motions as 'This Society deplores the recent growth of Trade Unions' (carried by eleven votes to one – Jack obviously did not present a convincing argument) and 'The Jacobite Rebellion of 1715 was more dangerous than that of 1745' (votes equal – a draw).[22]

As well as sport, Magdalen also placed a great emphasis on martial activities, particularly so in the years leading up to the First World War during Jack's time at the school. Drill had featured on the curriculum as far back as 1885 when ex-Army instructors came to the school on a part-time basis, but it was later considered that 'it is obviously necessary to have more drill',[23] so Magdalen appointed a full-time, resident, instructor in 1894 (a former soldier named Lance-Corporal Coote), who was also responsible for teaching gymnastics.[24] Firing butts were built in the school grounds as well as an indoor range in the gym. There was weekly shooting practice which led to inter-school and inter-house matches, the most popular being an annual competition between the boarders (house) and day-boys (town) over twenty-five and fifty yards, with team trophies and individual medals duly awarded to the winners.[25] In 1911, some fifteen boys shot at the National Rifle Association's annual camp at Bisley, and in 1914 Magdalen, Brackley, entered a team for the Senior Imperial Challenge Shield, open to teams of boys under nineteen years of age from all parts of the Empire.[26] Lidsey proved to be a decent shot, competing for both his house and the school during his latter years at Magdalen. There was also a school company which, it was hoped, would become a cadet corps and then, in time, an officer training corps.[27]

Some records of Jack's academic prowess while at Magdalen have survived, and it is fair to say that he was a far from outstanding scholar. *The Brackleian* published a league table of curricular achievement, called the Roll Order, on a termly basis, which showed a pupil's position in the school overall; within his form overall; and by individual subject within his form. At the start of his second school year, the October term of 1908, Lidsey was placed sixty-second out of seventy-eight boys in the school, and in his form, Form II, he came in at fifteenth out of nineteen pupils. In the individual subjects within Form II, he was ranked as follows:

Latin: 18th
French: 6th (not as successful as it appears – he was taking French
with the form a year below him)
Divinity: 18th
Mathematics: 15th
History: 15th
Geography: 14th equal
English: 15th
Science: 14th.

By the end of the 1910 school year, the last time that the Roll Orders
were published, he was ranked seventeenth in his form, Form III, again
out of nineteen pupils. In all the Roll Orders from 1908 to 1910, whether
by individual subject or overall, Jack is towards the foot of the rankings,
only very rarely making it into the upper half of the subject lists.[28]

For one who was so consistently poor in Divinity, Lidsey was,
however, one of fifteen boys who were confirmed in the school chapel
on 16 March 1911, when Bishop Mitchinson of Pembroke College, Oxford,
presided over the event. It was, says *The Brackleian*, 'a day which will long
live in the memory of most of us – a day which many of our number,
we confidently hope, will never forget'.[29]

The legal school leaving age had been set in 1899 at twelve years old,
but for a grammar school pupil to leave at so young an age would have
been very unusual – boys were expected to stay and complete examinations, and perhaps go on to higher education. At the time, there was no
nationally recognised, government-regulated, system for assessing
educational attainment – the School Certificate was not introduced until
1918 – so schools approached universities for local means of assess-
ment. Magdalen College School, Brackley, unsurprisingly, took its exams
under the auspices of the University of Oxford Delegacy of Local
Examinations, which had been established in 1857. The Delegacy set
exams for the pupils at the Preliminary, Junior, and Senior levels, which
were held every July in Brackley Town Hall[30], and there was also a Higher
Local level, a matriculation exam for university entrance. In Jack Lidsey's
case, he left school on 15 March 1913 when he was seventeen, after taking
his Senior level exams.[31] How well or otherwise he did in the tests is not

recorded, but his academic results prior to then were far from encouraging. Lidsey maintained his links with the school after leaving, serving on the committee of the old boys' society, the Old Brackleians, and playing cricket for them in the annual match against the School XI.[32]

Having come from a long line of farmers, it is reasonable to expect that Jack's father probably wanted him to follow the family path, and would have passed Hardwick Farm on to him in due course as his eldest son and heir. Whatever his motives, though, Jack chose not to go into farming, instead becoming articled as a trainee auctioneer and valuer at a Brackley firm owned by Harry Stace, who dealt with land, property and livestock sales in the local area from offices on the town's market place. Lidsey passed the preliminary examination for the Auctioneers' Institute in 1913,[33] shortly after leaving school, and could have chosen to take further qualifications under the Auctioneers' Institute or the Royal Institute of Chartered Surveyors once he had established himself. He would have been expected to work his way up from the bottom of the business's ladder, watching and learning from Harry Stace and the other auctioneers until they felt satisfied that he was ready to wield the gavel himself. Even then, he would not have been entrusted with selling the more lucrative lots, but rather those items left over at the end of the auction, such as eggs and rabbits, or the less desirable items of property. Brackley hosted a weekly livestock market and had permanent animal pens on the market place, and there was an annual Fat Stock Show each December. The market place was fertile ground for the auctioneers to cultivate relations with the local landowners and farmers for future sales in all departments. Furthermore, Lidsey's nearby home of Banbury was the location of the largest livestock market in the whole of Great Britain (and later, Europe), so it is easy to imagine that he spent time at auction there while apprenticed, especially as it was close to Hardwick House. He may well have gone to market with his father, a familiar attendee at the sales, who could cast an expert farmer's eye over the beasts on offer.

Jack Lidsey had only just settled himself into his chosen vocation when the storm clouds began to gather over Europe. War was not far away, and conflict with Germany finally came on 4 August 1914. The Michaelmas edition of that year's *The Brackleian* reflected the nation's mood in its editorial:

It is difficult for many of us to realise that the term through which
we have been passing marks the commencement of a new world
era. We have performed our ordinary tasks. Our routine of work
and play has been almost the same as ever. Devastated Belgium and
the blood-stained fields of Flanders seem far distant from us, in the
heart of rural England. Not that the true spirit of patriotism is
lacking amongst us! We are proud to publish in these pages a list
of Old Brackleians who are serving their King and Country. It is a
list in keeping with the traditions of the old School. And what, we
may ask, is there for us to do, who are left behind? There remains
steady work, an unceasing zeal in our own particular activities,
and unshakeable faith in our nation, its ideals and its ultimate
triumph.[34]

One of those names of serving old boys that appeared in the magazine's
list was that of William John Lidsey.

Chapter Two

1/4 (Oxfordshire) Battalion, The Oxfordshire & Buckinghamshire Light Infantry

The county of Oxfordshire first raised an infantry regiment in 1755. Numbered as the 52nd Regiment of Foot, the name 'Oxfordshire' was added to its title in 1782. The 52nd served throughout the British Empire; during the American War of Independence it fought at the battles of Lexington and Bunker Hill, where it stood alongside the 43rd (Monmouthshire) Regiment of Foot, with both regiments taking heavy casualties. The 52nd and the 43rd were selected by Sir John Moore to be, along with the 95th Rifles, the founding regiments of his new Light Brigade in 1803. Moore was widely considered at the time to be a fine soldier and the best trainer of troops that the British Army had ever had, so to be hand-picked by him to form his brigade was indeed an honour. Action in the Peninsular Wars and at Waterloo followed, after which General Sir William Napier, historian of the Peninsular Wars, wrote of the 52nd that it was 'a regiment never surpassed in arms, since arms were first borne by men'. Both regiments were in India during the Mutiny of 1857–59, where the first Victoria Crosses for each were won.

In 1881, the British Army underwent significant reforms under the then Secretary of State for War, Hugh Childers, who continued the earlier work done by his predecessor, Edward Cardwell. Under Childers, the 43rd and 52nd Regiments of Foot combined on 1 July that same year, forming the first and second battalions respectively of the newly created Oxfordshire Light Infantry, with its depot at Cowley Barracks on the outskirts of Oxford. Childers also called for each county regiment to have two militia (the official military reserve of the time) battalions.

Since the Oxfordshire Light Infantry's geographical sphere of influence also covered neighbouring Buckinghamshire, the Royal Bucks (King's Own) Militia became the 3rd (Militia) Battalion of the new regiment, with the Oxfordshire Militia forming the 4th (Militia) Battalion. Alongside the militia was the Volunteer Force, an autonomous citizen army of part-time riflemen; Childers' reforms brought these units under the control of the regular Army, and as such the 2nd Oxfordshire Rifle Volunteers became a volunteer battalion of the Oxfordshire Light Infantry, along with the 1st Buckinghamshire Rifle Volunteers.

Further changes came in 1908 under Richard Haldane, who, during his tenure at the War Office, created the Territorial Force for home defence. These latest reforms essentially abolished the existing county rifle volunteer and yeomanry (cavalry) units and merged them into the new force. As for the militia, it became the Special Reserve, and twenty-one of its battalions were declared redundant, one of which was the Oxfordshire Light Infantry's 3rd (Militia) Battalion, the Royal Bucks (King's Own) Militia, and it was duly disbanded. The regiment's new 3rd (Reserve) Battalion was then created by renumbering the 4th (Militia) Battalion.

The 2nd Oxfordshire Rifle Volunteers now became the regiment's 4th (Oxfordshire) Battalion, part of the new Territorial Force, which left the question of what to do with the 1st Buckinghamshire Rifle Volunteers, who now faced the prospect of being renamed as the 5th Battalion, the Oxfordshire Light Infantry. Such was the strength of feeling among the people of Buckinghamshire about the prospect of losing their county's name from the military lexicon that the entire regiment was renamed as The Oxfordshire and Buckinghamshire Light Infantry, with the Buckinghamshire Rifle Volunteers being given the title of 1st (Buckinghamshire) Battalion within the regiment (henceforth becoming the Ox & Bucks' second Territorial Force battalion), retaining their own cap badge, black buttons (distinctive of a rifle regiment), customs and individuality.

The 4th (Oxfordshire) Battalion was comprised of eight companies, lettered from A to H, and had its headquarters in St Cross Road in Oxford. Each company was based in various towns throughout the county, giving the battalion a truly pan-Oxfordshire recruiting base. A, B and H

Companies were based in the city of Oxford itself, while D Company, centred on Henley-on-Thames and Culham, covered the south and east. C and G Companies were in Banbury, with detachments at Brackley and Bicester, to the north of the county. Lastly, E and F Companies took in the western area, based in Chipping Norton and Witney respectively, with detachments in several Cotswold towns. The Brackley contingent of C Company was commanded by Second Lieutenant (later Major, Distinguished Service Order and Military Cross) Percival Pickford, assistant master and 'energetic' science teacher at Magdalen College School, Brackley, in his day job, and who would have been well known to Jack since Pickford was the master of Lovel House at the school when Lidsey was the house captain. Pickford later compiled the War Record of the Oxfordshire Battalion, referenced throughout this book.

When the First World War began on 4 August 1914, not everyone believed the popular notion that it would be over by the Christmas of that year. Lord Kitchener, then Secretary of State for War, foresaw a protracted and bloody campaign against a determined enemy and realised that Britain's small but professional Army would not be large enough to withstand great losses over an extended period of time. Kitchener immediately set about raising a new Army of civilian volunteers to augment the regulars, but recruiting, equipping and training such a large number of men could not happen overnight, and bringing them up to standard was inevitably going to take some time. Kitchener envisaged this New Army (or 'Kitchener's Army', as it was popularly known) being ready for combat in mid-1916, some two years away (although circumstances were to dictate its first use in September 1915 at the Battle of Loos).

In the meantime, there was the option of using the Territorial Force to fill the gap, but using this reserve Army presented problems of its own. The 'weekend volunteers' of the Territorial Force had signed up for home defence only, at a time before global conflict had been foreseen, and therefore could not be compelled to fight overseas, and in any case, many of them were under the minimum age of nineteen years old to be sent abroad. Territorial Force battalions were also generally under-strength (recruitment and retention had proved problematic since the force's creation), and furthermore they lacked the modern equipment of their regular counterparts, who had first call on new kit, particularly so in the case of rifles and artillery.

Reputation and a large degree of snobbery by the regular Army (which preferred conscription over part-time soldiers) also counted against the volunteers; for his part, Lord Kitchener was scornful of the fighting quality of Territorial Force units, his opinion having been tainted by the poor performance of their French equivalents during the Franco-Prussian War over forty years earlier. Of the part-time British Territorials, he said that they were 'led by middle-aged professional men who were allowed to put on uniform and play at soldiers'[35]. He would have preferred to have left the Territorial Force to do what it had been raised for – home defence – but operational necessity overrode Kitchener's prejudices. As early as 13 August 1914, just over a week after the declaration of hostilities, he agreed to deploy overseas those Territorial Force battalions in which at least eighty per cent (reduced to sixty per cent by the end of the month) of the volunteers had signed the Imperial Service Obligation, meaning that they were prepared to go to France and fight. Before the war, only around seven per cent of the reservists had taken the Obligation, but by the end of September 1914 that figure had risen tenfold.

The Oxfordshire Battalion had arrived for its annual training camp, which was due to last for a fortnight, at Great Marlow in Buckinghamshire on Sunday 2 August 1914. Everyone knew that war was imminent, and the very next day the battalion was recalled to its depot in Cowley where the men were dismissed with orders to be ready to mobilise at a moment's notice. The mobilisation order arrived at 5.00 p.m. on the 4th, the day that Great Britain declared war on Germany. The following morning, at 7.00 a.m., the battalion mustered at Cowley, from where the troops were sent off to various billets in Oxford. Over the next few days, the officers were 'delightfully quartered and feted in different colleges'[36] throughout the city, notably Keble, Balliol, Christ Church and New College, but for the other ranks, things were not quite so luxurious; Private (later Second Lieutenant, Military Cross) W.R.H. Brown said that they were crowded into the large dining hall at Balliol College, where they made themselves 'as comfortable as possible on a hard floor without proper sleeping accommodation'[37] – a portent of things to come. Fortunately, the university was empty of undergraduates for the summer holidays. By the late afternoon of the 5th, the battalion was fully mobilised and ready to move if need be.

On the evening of 9 August, orders were received detailing the Oxfordshires to move by train to an 'unknown destination'[38]. Cheering crowds gathered at the city's railway station to wave them off, with excited speculation rife about where they might be heading. The train shuddered to a halt less than an hour later, however, and the troops discovered, with some disappointment, that they had arrived only in Swindon, where the battalion was to become part of the 48th (South Midland) Division, a division made up entirely of Territorial Force battalions. Here, the men were asked if they wanted to sign the Imperial Service Obligation; more than eighty per cent of them volunteered to do so, and they were accordingly declared a Foreign Service Battalion. Those who took the Obligation were given the new collective identity of 1/4 (Oxfordshire) Battalion, confirming them as a first-line unit. The remainder who chose to stay behind as home service only, or who were ineligible for overseas deployment for whatever reason, were numbered as 2/4 Battalion, indicating a second-line organisation. The Ox & Bucks' other Territorial Force battalion, the 1st (Buckinghamshire), was similarly renumbered, becoming 1/1 and 2/1 Battalion respectively. The 1/1 Buckinghamshires joined the 1/4 Oxfordshires in the South Midland Division, and both were allocated to the division's 145 Brigade, along with the 1/5 Gloucestershires and 1/4 Royal Berkshires. The fates of these four battalions were to be entwined over the coming years of the war.

Since around twenty per cent of their complement were to remain at home, a lightning recruitment drive was launched throughout the county during the latter half of August to bring the 1/4 (Oxfordshire) Battalion up to full war strength. The campaign was extremely successful, and very quickly produced the quantity of men required. One of those new recruits was Jack Lidsey, who volunteered in Oxford. Along with the records of many servicemen of the First World War, his attestation papers no longer survive (they were destroyed by German bombing during the Second World War), but Lidsey was given the service number of 2438, an early serial indicating that he joined up towards the end of August and was therefore one of the first to respond to his country's call to arms. Jack could have joined Kitchener's New Army, but probably chose the Oxfordshire Battalion out of loyalty to his home county and also the influence of his old teacher, Pickford (the battalion was a popular choice among those Old Brackleians who joined up early in the war – *The Brackleian*'s list of Michaelmas 1914 referenced earlier, records thirteen of them serving alongside Lidsey). He perhaps also saw it as a quicker route to the war because the Territorial Force had already mobilised, whereas the New Army was still gathering recruits.

If the volunteers of the Oxfordshires had expected to go overseas straight away, they were to be sorely disappointed. The perceived threat of invasion by Germany kept them at home, marching to various locations around the countryside, first in Hertfordshire, then Bedfordshire, and then into Essex where they eventually ended up at Writtle, a village two miles west of Chelmsford, by the end of August. It was here that Jack Lidsey and the rest of the new recruits arrived to join their comrades. Again, the expectation was that the stay in Essex would be a short one and that the Oxfordshires would leave for France almost immediately, but they stayed encamped at Writtle for the next seven months, being trained for war. Sadly, Lidsey's diaries for this period of his service have long since been lost, so we do not know what he thought of life at the camp, although a remark from his brother Richard tells us that he 'was ever at loggerheads' with his bête noire, the company sergeant major, since he was 'averse to discipline'.

The Writtle regime was 'strenuous but congenial'[39], and they were welcomed 'royally'[40] by the local population, probably due in no small part to the extra income that the soldiers injected into the village economy. There was little free time, though, and over that autumn and winter a great deal of effort was made to improve the physique and stamina of the men. Time was spent doing physical training – including football, hockey, cross-country running and boxing – and there was a weekly route march that increased steadily in length until they could cover twenty-five miles without too much difficulty, and with not too many men falling out.

The battalion's military skills were honed too. They practised digging trenches and night operations, and spent long days in the field on manoeuvres. Marksmanship and musketry were taught and tested on the ranges at nearby Boreham or Purfleet; for field firing, a round trip

of three days by train to Dunstable Downs brought a welcome change
of routine. New kit was issued to replace the older style of equipment
that they had been given previously; assembling the webbing proved
tricky, with plenty of trial and error before it was put together to the
instructors' satisfaction. The troops were inoculated, and there was what
seemed an endless round of medical examinations, which resulted in
several disappointed men being sent home for a variety of seemingly
minor ailments. There were also proper military tasks to be carried out,
such as guarding the local wireless stations against – who knew what?
What precious leisure time the men had was spent either in the pub or
visiting Chelmsford. They went to the cathedral on Sundays and the
cinema during the week, as well as to the local YMCA hut. On 14 October,
the entire division paraded in nearby Hylands Park to be inspected by
His Majesty King George V.

Inevitably, the rumours about where the battalion would be sent began
to ferment. First it was definitely to be India, and then most certainly
Egypt, to relieve regular Army garrison troops who could then be sent
to France. But as the autumn of 1914 turned into winter, they found themselves still firmly rooted in Essex. The 'over by Christmas' cliché began
to have a detrimental effect on the morale of Jack and the other
Oxfordshires, and as 1914 drew to a close they feared they would miss
their chance to join in the war; they were 'incredibly jealous of the London
Scottish and other, more favoured, Territorial Battalions'[41] being sent
over to France before them. They need not have worried, though, since
1915 arrived with the war still going on and no end to it in sight.

Their frustrations inevitably spilled over into violence one night when
around 150 men were re-billeted from comfortable local houses into a
disused brewery malthouse, where they had no privacy, poor cooking
facilities, basic ablutions, and were crammed together to sleep on bags
of straw on bare floors. On their first night in the malthouse, many of
the men, who had been out drinking in the local pubs, rioted;
'pandemonium reigned supreme', according to Private Brown, and things
became 'very rough'[42]. The Military Police were called to arrest the ring-
leaders, but the mob put up such a fight that the MPs were forced to
withdraw. A civilian special constable then tried – somewhat foolishly
since he was alone – to restore order and was promptly bundled down

the steps by the scruff of his neck and thrown out of the building, his exit cheered drunkenly by the men inside. Even the intervention of the company commander failed – he could not make himself heard over the commotion – so things were then left to calm down by themselves. Next morning, the men were paraded in front of the battalion CO, Lieutenant Colonel Stockton, who threatened them with summary punishment if there was a repeat of their behaviour. The protest did have some success, though, and the malthouse barracks received baths, a canteen and a piano shortly afterwards.

In January 1915, the Oxfordshire Battalion underwent a reorganisation, changing from an eight- to a four-company structure to bring them in line with the regular and New Armies. A and B Companies combined to become A Company, with C and G becoming B. The new C Company (where Jack found himself) was formed by merging F and H, while D and E amalgamated to become D Company. Horses were also issued at this time to the company commanders, some of whom were not experienced riders, leading to 'many amusing episodes relating to horses and senior officers',[43] no doubt to the delight of the rank and file.

Then, on 27 March 1915, came the news that they had waited so eagerly for – 1/4 (Oxfordshire) Battalion, The Oxfordshire and Buckinghamshire Light Infantry, was to leave for France immediately. The advance party of two officers and eighty-four other ranks departed on the 28th, followed by the remainder of the battalion on the 29th. As they marched proudly out of Writtle Camp that evening for Chelmsford, from where they would entrain for the coast, 'the entire population assembled around the Green to see us off and wish us well, and we left behind a very discontented surplus of 100 men, mostly under nineteen, who were to join us a few months later'[44]. At 11.00 p.m. that night, 29 officers and 991 other ranks (including 2438 Private W.J. Lidsey) of the 1/4 Oxfordshires embarked aboard the SS *Onward*, a fast passenger steamer, at Folkestone.

Departing under the cover of darkness as soon as the last man was aboard, the *Onward* was escorted across the English Channel by a Royal Navy destroyer that circled the troopship throughout the voyage to deter any lurking enemy submarines; but the crossing was uneventful. They arrived and disembarked at Boulogne at 2.50 a.m. the following morning, the 30th. For the majority of the men, it was the first time they had been on foreign soil, and there was a mixture of anticipation, excitement and, most probably, apprehension. From the quayside, they were once again put on a train, their first experience of the French rail wagons labelled '*Hommes 40, Cheveaux 8*' that were to become all too familiar to them in the coming years.

Chapter Three

The Ypres Salient, April – June 1915

The virgin soldiers of the Oxfordshire Battalion were immediately sent eastwards, towards the Ypres Salient in Belgian Flanders. The Salient had formed in the late autumn of 1914 when the frantic manoeuvres of the opposing armies had coagulated into trench warfare, leaving the strategically important city of Ypres in British hands despite being surrounded on three sides and overlooked from the high ground all around. The First Battle of Ypres had already been fought, and it seemed inevitable that it would not be the last.

The battalion's first proper billet overseas was at a farm close to the village of Steenvoorde, just on the French side of the border with Belgium, around thirteen miles west of Ypres itself. Arriving there around midnight on All Fools' Day, 1 April, they discovered that their local guides had disappeared for the night, leaving the Oxfordshires to fend for themselves. Their lodgings were on the upper floor of a large barn, which they shared with cattle (the barn's usual residents) on the ground floor. The building was a potential death trap since it had only one small exit from the top storey in the gable end, from which the ground was reached by a long ladder. Given that the barn's floors were stuffed with straw over a foot thick, that their lighting was from naked candles, and that almost every man smoked, escape would have been impossible if there had been a blaze. It took the inexperienced troops a considerable time to bed themselves down, and they spent a cold night sleeping in the frost.[45]

Their arrival did not go unnoticed, however, and the next day they were inspected by General Sir Horace Smith-Dorien, commander of the British Second Army of which the battalion was now a part. It was at Steenvoorde that the men of the Oxfordshires first heard an ominous rumbling noise – the sound of British artillery fire sending shells towards the enemy front line. As they practised with their rifles and bayonets, it was all too apparent that the war was not far away and that they would soon be in it.

The battalion marched a short distance south on 4 April to new billets near Merris, close to Hazebrouck, before moving again to Nieppe, just outside Armentières. Jack was detailed to the battalion's transport section for the move, and drove a pair of mules bareback, pulling machine guns, for ten miles. When they arrived at their new destination, Lidsey, nursing a 'very sore sit-upon', was billeted with some of his comrades in the cellar of a house, and it was here that he had his first taste of war:

> At about 10am our artillery took up positions about 500 yards from our billet and fired all morning. At 12 noon the enemy sent 7 shells which landed in the field next to us where we were grazing our horses; first time we were under fire. Two of the 7 shells did not explode. At about 2.30pm 24 shells landed about 400 yards short of our billet, one hitting a house which fell like a pack of cards, and the bricks and timber flew up in the air like leaves in the wind. Another shell went through the roof of Ploegsteert church which was later shelled to stones. Women and children leaving the village in haste.

Company by company, the Oxfords went into the reserve and support trenches in Belgium around Ploegsteert Wood (or 'Plug Street', as the Tommies christened it) alongside seasoned troops who were already resident there, to learn from them and gain vital experience of trench warfare. Working with the men of the London Rifle Brigade, Jack 'received some valuable hints from a sergeant' when it was C Company's turn; they went to 'within 400 yards of the firing line', he observed in his diary with a hint of excitement.

Lidsey's introduction to the front line came on Saturday 10 April 1915. He had spent the morning erecting barbed-wire defences and had been on the receiving end of twenty German shells that fell in the field adjacent to his billet. Ever the farmer's son, Jack noted indignantly that the shells 'spoilt a nice field of wheat'. C Company was sent up the line at 7.30 p.m. that evening, arriving in the fire trench where they came under the wing of the East Lancashires, who were 'very considerate' to them. The territorials of the Oxfordshires regarded the East Lancs with a degree of hero-worship as they were regulars and had been overseas since the start of the war, part of that initial deployment of the British Expeditionary Force that came to be known as the 'Old Contemptibles' after a jibe by the Kaiser. For the first time, Lidsey found himself a direct target for enemy artillery; his trench was 'shelled vigorously'. He also got his first look at the 'Hun' when he 'saw two Germans bob up from their trench which was about 80 yards away, whilst looking through a periscope'. The next morning, the war was brought home sharply to the Oxfordshires when Private J.H.R. White, a 19-year-old from Banbury and a member of C Company's 12 Platoon, 'was shot through the neck and killed instantly', becoming the 1/4 Battalion's first man to be killed during the First World War.

It had been an eventful twenty-four hours when they moved out of the line and marched back to Nieppe, but the Oxfordshires had been blooded and were anxious to take over trenches of their own and help to win the war. After a hard, hot slog on roads of loose stones, they at least found a comfortable barn to sleep in, and a nearby brook in which to soak their aching feet. Jack, however, managed to pick up a virus from the water, no doubt borne from the nearby corpses of cattle and men, and spent the next two days in bed with stomach cramps. Good news reached him as he sweated out his bug, though – on 14 April he was promoted to lance corporal, making him second in command of his section.

Still suffering from the effects of a stomachful of dirty water, Lidsey and the Oxfordshires moved back up to Ploegsteert Wood on the 17th, this time taking over trenches from the Argyll & Sutherland Highlanders in an area known as Prowse Point on the northern side of the wood. After their baptism of fire a few days before, this stay in the line proved uneventful, with most of their time taken up with fatigues and working parties to improve the defences. Detailed to fetch up the day's water ration for C Company on the 21st, Jack overheard a man dressed in the uniform of the Royal Engineers 'questioning men concerning the position of artillery batteries'. His suspicions aroused, Lidsey promptly arrested the man, who was put under armed guard and marched away for questioning.

Every couple of days, the Oxfords would move back into hutted billets in Ploegsteert Wood itself, before returning to Prowse Point for another day or two in the line. The Germans shelled them constantly, both at the front line and at the rear areas in the woods. On 25 April, Jack sampled shrapnel shells for the first time when around thirty of them burst close by, an experience he was keen not to repeat, observing 'the first we have seen – don't want to see any more'. But it was not to be – regular shelling by all types of munitions were part and parcel of life in the trenches. That same afternoon, five heavy German shells burst within thirty yards of his tambour[46] causing the platoon to take cover until early evening when they decided that it was safer to be in the trench rather than the prominent fortification. The trench proved to be no less dangerous, though, as it was at right-angles to the trenches it connected to, and consequently attracted fire from two directions. Added to this, the trench was still being completed and had a low parapet in places, thus exposing them to the enemy.

Back in the support line on the eastern edge of Ploegsteert Wood, facing an enemy sector known as the Birdcage, Lidsey was fast becoming used to the routine: 'Marched into Ploegsteert Woods, within about 100 yards of the firing line and in direct line of fire; very dangerous when out of the shelter. Had a good strip-out bath in a "Jack Johnson"[47] hole and changed clothes and burnt old ones – first change in France.[48] Rather exciting time; plenty of bullets rattling in hedge just behind me. Watson wounded.'

Two days later, on 30 April, the Germans sent over '64 shells' in ten minutes in the early afternoon, and a few more for good measure later. Enemy snipers were also a constant danger, but the British had a marksman of their own: 'In the trenches there is a lovely snipering loophole, but only one man is allowed to shoot out of it – a Highlander. He has already accounted for 20 Bosches. There is a German sniper worrying our own men somewhere, so yesterday the Highlander went out with two days' rations; he is going to round the sniper up and is confident of doing so. There is also a German sniper somewhere who fires at night; his shots go over our tambour. He fires towards our trench every quarter of an hour absolutely regularly all night.' Whether or not the mysterious Highlander succeeded in stalking his prey, Jack did not record.

By now, the Second Battle of Ypres was raging just to the north of Ploegsteert, with the Germans attempting to destroy the Salient and capture Ypres itself. Poison gas, in the form of chlorine, had been used on the battlefield for the first time just a few days before; the attack had succeeded in routing the French colonial troops it had been directed against, but Canadian soldiers had rushed to fill the gap in the line just in time, preventing a German breakthrough that could have seen Ypres fall and possibly Germany win the war. The fear of gas attacks spread among the British troops, who as yet had little to counter the effects other than to hold urine-soaked socks over their mouths and noses. On 2 May, Lidsey and the rest of 10 Platoon were roused from their billets at 11.30 p.m. and ordered to rush to the trenches 'with liquid to counter-act the German gas shells, also water'. An enemy attack was expected at any moment and the Oxfordshires stood-to all night, with orders that no officer was to go to sleep and that each man was to be issued with a respirator pad and goggles[49] – the pad was to be worn on the forehead when the men slept in the fire trenches, ready for immediate use. Enemy movement was seen opposite the Oxford's trenches, prompting a belief that an attack was imminent; the German trenches were just forty yards away from the British positions. They stood-to, alert and waiting, every night for the next week. But the Germans did not come.

Sunday 9 May heralded a show of force by the British as a deception tactic to divert enemy attention away from an Allied assault on the Aubers Ridge that was about to start further south. The 'demonstration', as it was called, began with an artillery barrage at 4.30 a.m., followed by machine-gun fire towards the German trenches, interspersed with volleys of rifle fire, mortars and rifle grenades. The Oxfords 'carried on rapid firing all day. Ours and their machine guns "talking" all day long and exchanged many grenades.' Artillery fire raged on into the night, and the duel lasted another two days with the Germans often responding in kind.

The German artillery was being directed from an observation tower that the enemy had built from sandbags around 200 yards opposite the Oxfordshires' trenches. Battalion HQ decided to destroy the tower, so a

Royal Garrison Artillery mountain gun, most probably from an Indian battery, was brought into the front-line trench on 11 May. Mountain guns were specifically designed to be broken down for ease of transportation (mostly by mules on remote mountain passes), and were therefore smaller than standard field pieces, so it was relatively easy to assemble and position one within the trench. At 3.30 a.m. the next morning, the mountain gun opened fire on the tower, bringing it crashing down, to the great delight of the British infantry. The Germans responded with a volley of rifle grenades, one of which landed in the middle of the Oxfordshires' trench, killing Captain Ernest Dashwood, the CO of B Company (he had only taken over the company the day before, following the wounding of the previous CO, Captain Rose), and wounding four others including Second Lieutenant Cranmer. Dashwood was the 1/4 Battalion's first officer to be killed in the First World War; he was the son of the 6th Baronet Dashwood, and his brother Lionel was killed just five days later. Another sibling was to die later in the war, and two more survived.

The work of either digging or improving the trenches and defences continued, often with the enemy doing the same thing just yards away, 'neither party attempting to molest the other'[50]. Hot late spring weather made the work arduous and tiring, and the pace was relentless. The Oxfords by now considered themselves expert trench builders, and very proficient at barbed-wire defences. Lidsey spent all day on 14 May working on wire entanglements – the technique used was to make so-called 'knife rests' from timbers which were then thrown over the trench parapet into no-man's-land to be wired together at night when it was safer to work. Even so, Jack had a couple of near misses while on wiring duty; on the 15th he was hit in the forearm by a piece of shrapnel, which left a 'nasty bruise', and the next day he and another man had decided to go souvenir hunting, looking for shell heads, when the Germans turned a machine gun on them, sending them sprawling into a shell hole for cover. They pressed themselves flat to the ground for five minutes and then 'got up and ran like hares; about the closest shave I have had'.

Deception 'demonstrations' were not just the preserve of the British. On 23 May, as the Second Battle of Ypres reached its conclusion, the Germans launched just such an operation opposite the Oxfordshires' positions in Ploegsteert Wood. At dawn, the enemy sent over an artillery barrage, which was answered by British machine guns. Reports came in that the Germans were hoisting dummies on to their parapet to simulate going 'over the top', eliciting a furious rapid rifle-fire response from the British troops. Things quietened down as the sun rose and it was easier to see, but that night Lidsey was helping to build a sandbag parapet when 'a great shout came from the German trenches; thought they were charging. Great excitement; all rushed to our posts and fired rapid at them. Hundreds of star lights went up to see what was happening. Very good firework display; had to stand-to for two hours after'. No damage was done by either side, and the net result was a significant amount of wasted ammunition.

With a German attack still a possibility, Jack went out into no-man's-land the next night on a listening patrol to try to gather intelligence. At 11.30 p.m., he and a few others 'crawled out on all fours from our trench half-way across to the Bosche's trench'. All was quiet, though, and after two and a half hours, they slid back into their own trench, 'wet through with the dew and smothered with mud'.

As the month of May 1915 ended, so did the Second Battle of Ypres. The Germans had succeeded in compressing the Salient but had not managed to eliminate it. Ypres itself was still in British hands but by now was in ruins and much closer to the front line than before; no matter, though – the enemy had been held. For their part, the Oxfordshire Battalion had endured a protracted stay at the front, either in the fire trenches or in support, with only the odd few hours in the rear for a bath before going forward again. It had been a damaging residency, costing them ten killed and over thirty wounded.

The heatwave continued into early June, sapping the energy of the exhausted troops even further. Jack became ill, reporting to the doctor with a dose of 'wherry go nimbles', a delicate way of saying diarrhoea, which lasted on and off for three weeks. His twentieth birthday on 6 June was to prove memorable, however. For some time, the British had been tunnelling under the German trenches opposite Ploegsteert Wood but had detected the sounds of enemy counter-mining close by. Fearing that the Germans would blow up their mine first, the British decided to strike early. The Oxfords were detailed to send a working party to ferry five tons of gun cotton to the mine head in preparation for the detonation, and to keep the enemy's attention focused elsewhere, the rest of the battalion were ordered to march up and down on the roads to the rear of the fire trenches, making as much noise as possible. Finally, everything was ready:

> 20th Birthday; we had to have some celebrations. At 10.15am we blew the German sap up opposite us; legs, arms and machine-guns went up into the air about 100 feet. One German landed on our barbed wire; he was of course dead – he was blown up in the air about 200 feet. Curiously, his hat was still on; some men described him as the biggest man they had ever seen. As soon as the mine went up, our artillery shelled the trenches vigorously for about 15 minutes; in about 10 minutes the Bosches started shelling back and continued sending high explosive shells in all directions all day; not a single man or gun was touched. When the mine went off I was kneeling on the ground and distinctly felt the ground shake.

At last, after around forty days and nights in Ploegsteert Wood, the Oxfordshires were relieved. They marched back to Nieppe on 7 June, arriving 'absolutely done' in the heat, and with Lidsey's bowels continuing to plague him for the next couple of days. If the battalion was expecting complete rest, they were mistaken; the next few days were taken up with route marches and drill, culminating with a parade and inspection by the new commander of the 48th Division, Major General Robert Fanshawe, on the 10th.

The 'respite' was to prove all too short. On the 11th, the battalion moved back to Prowse Point to take their place in the line once more. They took over a section of the line from the Royal Warwickshires, slightly further north of where they had been before. As soon as they had gone into the trenches, Jack was ordered to accompany his platoon commander, Lieutenant Craig, out into no-man's-land to inspect the wire entanglements – it was broad daylight. Pressing himself to the ground, Lidsey crawled on his stomach out to the wire, willing himself to become part of the earth and praying not to be seen. The journey of 200 yards seemed interminable. Satisfied that the wire was intact, Craig whispered to Jack that they were going back. The two men slithered into the relative safety of the fire trench, wet through and caked in mud, relieved that the German trenches here were further away than they had been used to, making it harder for the enemy snipers to carry out their deadly business.

The now-familiar routine of being shelled began again. On 13 June, D Company took six casualties wounded when they were hit by shrapnel rounds, but fortunately none were killed. The next morning, at about 2.00 a.m., Lidsey was standing-to in his trench when the ground shook beneath him, followed immediately by heavy artillery and rifle fire from the German lines. Great clods of earth, rocks and stones began to rain down on him from above, and Jack quickly realised that the Germans had exploded a mine off to the right, aimed at the trenches the Oxfords had occupied previously. Thankfully the enemy tunnellers had miscalculated and come up about twenty yards short, saving the British trench from the worst of the detonation.

The next six days passed without major incident, with the cycle continuing of manning the fire trenches, followed by moving back in support and carrying out repair work, guarding, and fatigues under clear skies and hot sun. On 19 June, the Oxfords handed over to the Worcesters and went into huts back towards Nieppe, away from the front line once more. So ended the Oxfordshire Battalion's first period in the Ypres Salient; they did not go back into the line in the area for another two years. In the meantime, they were moved south into France. They ended June billeted in a school in Allouagne, just west of Béthune, leaving thirteen of their comrades behind in 'Plug Street' Wood – men of Oxfordshire, buried beneath the soil of Flanders.

Chapter Four

The Somme, July 1915 – February 1916

Three long and stiflingly hot route marches, followed by slow train journeys, took the Oxfords to Nœux-les-Mines, close to Lens, by the second week in July 1915. They spent their time training so that they could take over trenches in the area as soon as they were ready, but the order was cancelled. Instead, they carried on honing their battle skills and organising working parties. Lidsey also put his schoolboy French to good use by bartering with the local residents for food to supplement his platoon's daily rations, although he wasn't always entirely successful:

> The farmer had some very good onions and new potatoes which he would not sell, so we had to 'borrow' some; we took the spuds to his wife and paid her tuppence to cook them!! Next to our residence [a pig sty] was a jolly fine cherry orchard; the old man sold us cherries very cheap, consequently we were eating them all day; he and his wife could not pick them half quick enough – they were picking all day long!! In the evening tried my French very successfully over the wall with a little girl next door; in consequence I was a good supplier of lettuce and onions on the cheap, to say nothing of two or three handfuls of jolly fine white currants.

The British Army's early experiences in the war had shown the value of bombing in trench warfare[51], and the battalion spent a great deal of time learning how to use grenades effectively, including throwing live bombs during mock attacks. This realistic training was to prove fatal on 12 July, however; Lieutenant C. Vyner of A Company was demonstrating how to throw a Mills bomb when it exploded as soon as it left his hand. One man was killed outright by the blast and nine others were wounded, two of whom, including Vyner, later also died.

With the deployment into the Nœux trenches called off, the battalion was detailed to move again. Working their way southwards by a combination of trains, motor transport and foot-slogging, the Oxfordshires finally arrived at Coigneux, four miles west of Hébuterne in the Somme Valley. This part of France was to become well-worn and depressingly familiar to Jack and the Oxfords over the next year and a half, although they were not to know that yet. They arrived at their new billets, bivouacs in a field, on 19 July after yet another march in the summer heat. The French troops that they were relieving were still there when they arrived and were only too willing to trade souvenirs with their British allies, and Lidsey came away with rings made from aluminium and copper salvaged from shell cases.

Following a night's rest, the battalion took over the French trenches in front of Hébuterne, to the east of the village. After being so close to the enemy in Ploegsteert Wood, they were pleasantly surprised to find a quiet stretch of the line and the German fire trenches almost 800 yards away, out of sight. Things were so calm that Lidsey had 'the hardest job to prevent oneself from going to sleep'. Of course, the peace and quiet could not last, and it was not long before German artillery started shelling the new arrivals, causing the first casualties by wounding on the 22nd: 'At 6.0pm the Bosches dropped 6 heavy calibre shells into the village, very close to us; we were hit several times by bits of flying debris – no lives were lost, and it is impossible to do any more damage to the village itself as there are only two houses in the village that are not total ruins, and they are badly damaged; one of the two is the medical station, the other Battalion Headquarters.'

The next day, Jack reported sick, although he makes no mention of what was wrong, and spent the next three days at various medical facilities recovering. The cause of his illness could well have been the filthy condition of the trenches that the Oxfordshires had inherited, since the French troops had left them in an awful state, and the British found themselves dealing with rats and lice for the first time. The period immediately after breakfast soon became the soldiers' time for lice-hunting – shirts would be removed and the detested creatures killed by the dozen.

Hébuterne was to be turned into a redoubt and defended to the last man in the event of a German attack. When Lidsey returned to the battalion once he had recovered, he found the men hard at work, toiling at digging new trenches and, of course, building the inevitable barbed-wire defences to surround the village. The shelling grew worse, becoming a daily occurrence. On 28 July he 'watched the Bosches trying to find one of our artillery batteries; the shells screeched directly over us, bursting about 400 yards away. Nearly 200 shells came over in 15 minutes. During the afternoon 60 shells dropped just beyond the trench; not a soul was touched.' British artillery responded in kind, with Lidsey watching as the guns battered a 100-yard stretch of the German trenches; 'for about one minute, 50 shells fell. It must have been a perfect hell in that trench; practically every shell hit the parapet, and it was impossible to see the trench for black smoke after about half a minute.'

On the last day of July the few remaining French troops left the Hébuterne trenches, leaving everything to the British. As he was entering his shelter, Jack overheard a telephone conversation between his company CO and a French officer, a colonel. The Frenchman was telling his British counterpart that he did not want there to be any 'hate' (German shelling) until he had his men clear, evidently not wanting the British to stir anything up before he was well out of the way. The Germans soon realised who their new neighbours were, though:

Our trenches were shelled on and off all day; some very heavy shells fell, and four men were wounded and two burned but not hurt. Our nerves were jumping about all day long; it was the first time that we had been in a prolonged bombardment, and I don't want to be in another. Did nothing all day long but flop down flat in the bottom of the trench as we heard them screeching towards us. At night were relieved by A Company and moved to a brickyard about 30 yards behind the main trench; much more dangerous than being in the trench itself – when a shell hits the bricks, the bits of brick are as dangerous as the bits of shell.

After weeks of baking summer sunshine, the heavens opened on 2 August, bringing several days of continuous rain. Very quickly, the trenches became 'a beastly mess', and the men were 'wet through the whole time', even when under their shelter, which was 'by no means waterproof'. The British front line was on lower ground than that of the Germans, so water flowed downhill from the enemy positions into those of the Oxfords. The digging of new trenches had to continue, however, whatever the weather, if Hébuterne was to be defended. While they were labouring on the 5th, Jack's platoon was spotted by a German observation balloon and in quick time a shrapnel shell burst overhead. The only man injured was called Loveday, who had the misfortune to be 'performing the necessities of nature' when the shell came over and was hit in the back and wrist. Loveday reported to the platoon commander, Lieutenant Craig, saying 'I think they've hit me'; blood was pouring from his arm, an artery having been severed. There can surely be no greater ignominy for a soldier than to be hit while on the latrine.

The Oxfordshires left the front line that night and found new billets in a stable in the village of Sailly-au-Bois, some three miles away. Lidsey passed an 'uncomfortable night' on the rough stone floor but managed to buy some straw from the farmer next morning and transformed the billet into 'quite a comfortable residence'; just as well, since the rain continued to pour down. Jack watched the heaviest thunderstorm he had ever seen, with lighting so bright and consistent that 'it was quite easy to sit in the dark and read a book'. Rainwater ran a foot deep down the road for an hour. Dry inside his stable, Lidsey thanked his lucky stars that he was not in the trenches that night. They still weren't out of the danger area, though, and on Sunday 8 August, sixteen shells landed on Sailly, wounding five men of the Oxfords' machine-gun section. Despite the hazards, the battalion managed three days of complete rest, with no working parties to disrupt their respite.

But Lidsey was not to escape a turn in the trenches during a thunderstorm. Moving back into the line on Friday the 13th, he found that a 'thunderstorm in the morning made trenches a beastly mess. At night, 12.30am, I took out five men in front of our trench to see if any Bosches patrols were about and if so capture the same. Did not see any, got thoroughly wet through. Found a board stuck up 100 yards from our trench with the following inscription – "Warsaw fallen; London next". We did not touch it as such boards often have bombs attached which explode when the board is moved. German helmets are often 'doctored' in the same way so that we are very careful with any souvenirs we find between the lines.'

Another patrol a couple of days later came across the corpse of a German soldier lying in a shell hole in front of the British wire: 'I should think he had been there for over a month; he had no rifle, bayonet or helmet. They brought in his buttons, shoulder badges, leg strikes, ammunition, letters and pencils, and one boot with the foot in it; also, a rib and a bit of his shoulder. They were going to bring in the other boot with the leg in up to the thigh, but it smelt a bit 'high' so they decided to leave it.'

When it was their turn to leave the fire trench, 10 Platoon was sent to the dreaded brickyard to work on brick cleaning for the next few days, salvaging whatever bricks they could find to be used in building the Hébuterne defences and to pave the trench floors. It was hated work given the deadly brick splinters that would fly around whenever a shell landed; they would almost have preferred to have been back in the line. Along with the reclaimed bricks, they also used timbers from the destroyed houses in the village to build barricades in and around the streets. Hébuterne was fast beginning to resemble a fortress and had earned the nickname 'The Keep'. While they were working on the defences on the 27th, a shell landed in the brickyard, now occupied by a work party from the Berkshires, killing six men and wounding a further ten. For Jack and the rest of 10 Platoon, it had been a very lucky escape.

They took over a section of the line from the Glosters on 31 August, occupying trenches they had not been to before:

Left the village at 2.30pm. To get to the trenches we had to go up a two-and-a-half-mile long communication trench, a very bad one at that. The fire trench is a beastly, rotten place and we shall have the devil of a time if it rains; there are no decent dug-outs, and each man has to get into a cramped little hole scraped out of the wall of the trench or sleep on the firestep which is the most uncomfortable of the two. Our part of the trench is 300 yards from the Germans; in one place, the trenches are only 20 yards apart. A part of our trench is part of what was once a German trench before the French captured it on July 3rd; their dug-outs are marvellous downstairs, 20 or 30 feet into the ground. Am glad we are not in that part as there is a most beastly smell of dead bodies all through it.

Of course, it did rain that day and for the next two days, and the mud was calf-deep in the bottom of the squalid trench. The deluge caused the roofs of the dugouts to cave in; with nowhere to shelter or to dry out, the men were wet through and stayed that way. Relieved by the Warwickshires after two days, they headed back the way they had come, along the awful, interminable communication trench, which was now in an even worse state. It took them an hour and a half to wade their way through the mire back to the Keep. They grew to loathe that communication trench, since they were detailed to carry supplies back up it for the next two days, all the time in the pouring rain and with each footfall making the sludge deeper. By the time it was their turn in the fire trench again, it had been turned into a quagmire with the mud by now knee-deep. And still it rained.

Thankfully, the Oxfordshires' latest stint in the line lasted only twenty-four hours before they returned to Hébuterne down the long trench once more, practically having to swim through the mud to get back. They were billeted in another barn, this time in the nearby village of Courcelles-au-Bois, but despite being comfortable, the barn was full of lice from its previous equine inhabitants. The village, though, was well appointed, with football pitches and a concert hall, and the opportunity for a bath and laundry. There was even French beer to be had, although to the British troops, more used to English bitter, it seemed as thin as water. The chance to be rid of the stinking filth from the long trench was a luxury that they seized readily, and Jack revelled in having a new tunic and clean underwear. The rations were good, too; after a day of trench digging on 8 September, they 'did justice to a good meal of roast mutton', and there were still some French civilians in the village who were more than happy to sell food to the troops, with eggs and fried potatoes proving the most popular fare. The Oxfords spent ten days at Courcelles, digging trenches during the day and carrying out light training in the evenings. Although the days of work were long and tiring, they were at least away from the front and had use of everything that the village had to offer.

They moved back up into the line on Friday 17 September, into the same stretch of trenches as before, known as G Sector. Taking the old familiar and detested route along the long communication trench, they were almost at their destination when 'some idiot wanted to try the new trench or some such rot'. Taking a detour, they followed a roundabout route, eventually arriving where they should have been after a five-mile trek, which 'made us pretty well fed up', especially as they had been on a ten-mile route march in full kit just the day before. It was not a good way to begin. Jack managed to find a decent dugout, though, just big enough for one person, after discovering that the one he had used twelve days before had since collapsed in the rain.

By and large, this latest stay in the front line was relatively quiet. There was sporadic shelling from the Germans on most days, but by now the Oxfords had learned what was considered 'normal' or 'light', and what was 'heavy'. The bulk of the work was done in repairing and reinforcing the barbed wire; this was far too hazardous to carry out in daylight, so most nights were spent creeping over the parapet carrying coils of wire in front of the trench to where the entanglements were. One night, Jack was out for six hours working on the wire when he noticed three unexploded bombs close by. One was a British Pitcher grenade, 'very dangerous, guaranteed to kill at 200 yards'. The Pitcher was made live by pulling a length of tape out of the top of the grenade before throwing it, and this one had the tape exposed, but it evidently had not been pulled out hard or far enough. Edging gingerly away from the bomb, Lidsey no doubt thanked his lucky stars that he had not trodden on the tape in the dark, or that it had not got snagged and yanked out by a length of barbed wire. One of the other bombs was round, like a cricket ball, with a tube sticking out of it. Not having seen one like it before, he decided to bring it back in for the bomb specialists to take a look at. When he presented them with his find, they almost ran a mile; it was a French grenade, and the tube was the cocking mechanism that, when pulled out like the tape in the Pitcher, made the weapon live. The grenade experts told him that 'this bomb is very dangerous indeed; the English bombers will not touch them, and only very few Frenchmen will'.

On 25 September, the British launched a major offensive at Loos, around twenty-five miles north of Hébuterne, with the aim of breaking through the German front line and restoring movement, rather than static, trench warfare. Again, there was a diversionary artillery barrage from Allied artillery close to the Oxfordshires. The guns opened fire 'in a continuous roar; it was absolutely deafening; our artillery threw a thousand shells against the German positions', Lidsey remarked. The rumours began to flow, with stories that 'Lille and four other unnamed places have been taken by us'[52]. Before long, though, the truth filtered through. Jack 'heard that the French have been driven back and that the British 2nd Division had to evacuate their trenches due to exceptionally heavy shelling'. On the 26th, the Oxfords were warned that they were to attack the next day, to take some of the pressure off their beleaguered comrades to the north. The day was spent making 'great preparations; we expect to attack at daybreak tomorrow or sooner'. At 8.00 p.m., however, an order came through cancelling the operation indefinitely. The main attack at Loos had failed and although it stumbled on into early October, no substantial gains were made. By Monday the 27th, the artillery behind Jack's trench had gone quiet. And it was raining again.

The battalion moved back to their old quarters in Courcelles on the 29th, pleased to leave behind the 'six hardest days' work we have done since May'. Lidsey was sent away to Sailly on a ten-day bombing course, where he learned grenade tactics and threw both dummy and live bombs, as well as how to make improvised bombs from empty jam tins. On one of the days 'the Frenchman next door killed a pig, so I gave him 1 Franc for the brains, which the cook fried for supper – very *bon*! Also bought about 4 lbs of honey for 2 Francs; also very good.'

With the bombing course completed successfully, he returned to the battalion at Courcelles on 9 October, where he sought an interview with his company commander, Captain Coleman. Lidsey asked Coleman if he would recommend him for a commission, and Coleman replied that he 'would do so willingly'. Jack was the right sort of candidate to become an officer; he was a junior NCO with combat experience, was a former grammar school boy, and came from a good family. He evidently felt that he was destined for higher things, but there were several hurdles to overcome before then, though, and in the meantime, it was back to being Lance Corporal Lidsey.

Another five miles through the long communication trench and the warren of channels running off it took Jack back to the front line on the 11th. With winter fast approaching the routine changed, with only one platoon at a time in the fire trench whereas there had been a full company in the summer, and platoons swapping between the fire and support trenches every twenty-four hours. Possibly with an eye on his suitability for commissioning, Lidsey was put in charge of a six-man sentry post. Enemy activity was light, with just the occasional rifle grenade and bursts from machine guns; perhaps they too were busy preparing for another winter. The Oxfords responded in kind, often sending back more than they got.

Then one morning, Jack Lidsey's world changed forever:

Saturday October 16th
First thing after daybreak it was very misty; had to stand-to until 9am. At 7.30 the mist rose suddenly. We were in front of our wire searching for souvenirs and had to hurry in immediately as their trench was plainly visible. As soon as we were in, I spotted a German sniper in the grass in front of the German wire. He presented a good 'head and shoulder' target at 400 yards; I had one shot and down he went. About half an hour later another Bosche was seen running towards this one, evidently to fetch the first one in or see if there was any life in him. Our sentry spotted him and with a jolly fine shot filled him as he was running.

For the first time, he had killed a man.

Two days later, the quiet period finished:

During the morning the Bosches put about ten Jack Johnsons just behind our front trench. In the afternoon we were subject to very heavy shelling by 12, 6 and 5-inch guns; very trying to the nerves. Fortunately, their aim was not very good; only one shell doing any material damage, this falling on the signallers' dug-out. Captain Treble killed (cut all to pieces), Corporal Ruddle had bleeding concussion and will probably not survive,[53] and one Private is missing, evidently blown to atoms[54]. Trench 30 was rather badly damaged with several traverses being entirely destroyed.

So severe was the bombardment that the War Diary stated that 'Trench 31 was smashed almost flat and looked like a ploughed field. All the dug-outs practically smashed in. One man became demented and had to be taken out. Worst shelling we have had.'[55] The day was not over yet:

At 10pm we sent out a patrol of six men under a Corporal. They ran into a big German patrol who were lying in the grass waiting for them. The first our patrol knew of them was when the Germans opened rapid fire on them. The patrol did the only thing that was possible against such numbers – make for our trenches with all possible haste. One man – Simms – who had only joined us a few days previously, was hit. They were obliged to leave him as the fire was too hot to allow the others to stop and bring him in. Three men went out and brought him in several hours later. Upon examination it was found that he must have been killed instantly, one bullet passing through his head and another through his stomach.[56]

And so it continued the following day:

Tuesday October 19th
About dinner time the Germans sent six very powerful trench mortar shells into our trench, about 200 yards on our left. The explosion was about three times as great as that of a Jack Johnson shell. We could follow the trench mortar shells with our eyes all the way from their trench to ours. We phoned back to the artillery who sent about ten six-inch shells somewhere near the mortar – it did not fire again. The Seaforths who were on our right told us that the bombardment we had been subject to during the last two days was worse than that of Second Ypres, and that we should be unfortunate if we ever got into a hotter phase. It was an absolute miracle that we had so few casualties. Worcesters relieved us at 3.30pm; we returned to our billets at Courcelles very tired and jolly glad to be away from the trenches.

The next few days were spent on barbed-wire defences and digging dugouts around Coigneux, and playing several games of football. Making their way to a wiring fatigue on 21 October, Lidsey and his comrades met the divisional commander, Major General Fanshawe, who took their 'eyes right' salute as they marched past 'absolutely perfectly'. Evidently impressed, Fanshawe galloped back to the head of the column and shouted to the officer in charge, Lieutenant Edmonds, that 'they are marching splendidly and the men look well'. The general (nicknamed 'The Chocolate Soldier') had been an officer with the old Oxfordshire Light Infantry and had spent sixteen years, mainly in India, with the regiment; Jack mused that 'I'll bet he said to himself "my Oxfords again"' as they passed by.

On Monday 25th, the Oxfordshires, in concert with 'many thousands of troops', paraded at Acheux in front of King George V and President Poincaré of France, and were inspected by the monarch and his sizeable entourage. Lidsey declared it a 'grand sight, to see so many thousands of men all doing "Royal Salute" with fixed bayonets'. The Oxfordshire Battalion had been specially chosen by General Fanshawe to represent the 48th Division and were the only Territorial Force unit on parade, probably as a direct result of their impromptu march-past a few days earlier and the general's association with the regiment. The weather did not play its part on the day, however. Constant rain and freezing temperatures throughout made for a miserable time of it, compounded by the men not being permitted to wear greatcoats to protect themselves from the wet and cold during the parade – they had been told to take them off beforehand. They waited, shivering and exposed to the elements, for three hours until the King arrived, and then it was all over in a matter of minutes. Once he had left, they were allowed to put their coats back on, albeit over their sodden uniforms. The rain refused to let up, continuing throughout the rest of the month and on into November. On 27 October, the battalion was issued with winter underclothing and ordered back into the G Sector trenches. Conditions were dreadful; 'trenches fell in everywhere and incessant labour was necessary to keep any of them open at all; men stuck in the soft mud and literally had to be dug out'[57]. Jack wrote on 2 November that:

The rain of the last few days made the poor rotten old communications trench and fire trench collapse on both sides; it fell in all the way along except for just a few places where it was revetted. No shelling could possibly have made a bigger mess of the trenches. We had to work like niggers for 12 hours, most of the time up to our knees in the liquid mud, and very cold. It was about the hardest work I have ever done as the only way of getting rid of the earth was by throwing it up about five feet out of the trench; it was almost impossible to make the mud leave the shovel. What made matters worse was that our dug-out leaked like a sieve and we were lying in nearly an inch of water. During the night the roof slipped about a foot; I thought we were all going to be buried alive.

The hard labour continued until they were relieved on the 4th: 'Thank goodness, after having been wet through from above the knees downwards for six days and had not had our boots off for eight days. Feet very sore and chilled, through being cold and wet through for so long. Got back to Courcelles at 5.30pm; had a very welcome change of socks.'

With a modicum of comfort restored, Lidsey took the next step in his quest for a commission by writing to the Oxfordshires' former commanding officer, Lieutenant Colonel Stockton, to ask for his endorsement. Stockton had been in charge of the battalion at the outbreak of the war and would therefore have known Jack from the early days at Writtle, but perhaps more significantly he was also an Old Brackleian, a fact that Jack would have been aware of from his service on the society's committee before the war. Colonel Stockton's patronage would go a long way to ensuring the success of Lidsey's application. The usual round of working parties and route marches followed, interspersed with opportunities to feel human again. Mobile laundry and bathing services were available, and the Oxfordshires were fumigated, a 'very good job done; the Hitchy Koo[58] casualties were millions'. Jack also went to a concert party production and was very pleasantly surprised to find 'two English girls there, the first we had seen since leaving Boulogne in March last'.

The rain during that early November was incessant. Barely had they had time to get clean and dry than it was the Oxfords' turn in the line once more. On the 12th of the month they: 'Marched or rather paddled up to the trenches, up the 3 miles of communication trench up to our knees in water. In the evening went up to the fire trench on fatigue; stepped on a corduroy [59] that was not there and got into a sump hole up to my waist. Consequently, felt beastly rotten all night.'

As before, the trench sides were caving in under the weight of the rain. Those that had not given way already had 'two inches of water in the bottom', making sleep impossible. Finally, on the 14th, the rain stopped and the first cold of winter arrived, freezing everything. The Oxfords' fire trenches had no dugouts, so the men were constantly exposed to the elements. That night, Lidsey observed, was 'the most miserable night that I have ever had in the trenches', and then to make matters worse, it snowed early the next morning. The weather began to take its toll on the soldiers; Jack felt 'rotten and had a splitting headache', and others were hospitalised with jaundice. On the night of the 15th, the Germans carried out a raid on Lidsey's trench, throwing in a grenade that fortunately failed to explode. C Company opened fire as the enemy ran back to their own lines, but the mist and dark made it impossible to see if any were hit. An inspection showed that no damage had been done, although a second German grenade was found, apparently dropped in the enemy's hurry to get away.

The snow returned, a heavy fall dumping four inches of it the following night. Thankfully, C Company were sent into the reserve trenches where they were able to have a hot foot bath and breakfast. They were wet through and covered in mud – a 'beastly state to be in'. The men spent the day clearing the corduroys of snow before spending the night in a 'very cold stable; nearly frozen to death'. The rest of that period in the trenches was spent bringing supplies up from the rear, mainly at night, until they marched back to Coigneux on the 20th, where Jack felt that 'it is like coming back to home; had a glorious night's sleep in a blanket'. This spell behind the lines was mostly spent digging new trenches, which was considered to be 'a light day's rest'. Lidsey complained to his diary that trench-digging earned the sappers of the Royal Engineers 2s 8d per day, whereas infantrymen like him only collected their normal daily pay of 1s.

After another eight days at Coigneux and Courcelles, during which period it snowed again, they went back to G Sector once more. Conditions this time were no better, since a thaw had set in bringing torrential rain, reducing the trenches to the inevitable quagmire. In the fire trench, Jack found the water above his knees, and he stood there for the next sixteen hours with nowhere to sit down. They had a section of men from the Manchester Regiment with them under instruction who had had no food for over a day, so the Oxfords shared what they could of their own rations, adding to the misery and discomfort. At least enemy activity was light, even though the Germans had shouted across to the Oxfordshires that they were going to give them a 'hot time', which thankfully had not materialised. The days were spent pumping water and digging the trenches out, and labouring in waist-deep mud and water to try and shore up the walls of the collapsing earthworks. In places, the communications trenches were completely impassable, and 'trench foot' was becoming an increasing problem. Jack's platoon spent a welcome twenty-four hours out of the fire trench on 30 November, and he managed to wash his feet and massage them which 'did me the world of good', but by the evening they were in just as bad a state after four hours of 'pumping out sump holes, standing nearly waist-deep in mud and water. Was absolutely fed up and felt jolly rotten.' He reported sick the next morning; the medical officer gave him 'two cough pills and [light] duty; I blessed him. Had most of the day off, got a little sleep.'

By early December, despite their hard labour, the trenches were in an even worse state, with the dugouts either flooded or fallen in. Only one was remotely inhabitable, and the men were forced to 'get what shelter we could under sheets of corrugated iron stretched across the trench'. No sooner had they cleared one part of a trench than another would cave in – conditions began to get worse, with the communications trenches again impassable here and there, and the men 'absolutely unable to cope with the work'[60] of keeping them clear. The Oxfords were responsible for an eight-mile stretch of trench, and they were fighting a losing battle with the elements. On 2 December two men sank into the mud and had to be dug out, and the next day four men of B Company were killed and two more injured when their dugout collapsed in on them. Men took to moving around in the daylight, something not normally undertaken due to the risk of being shot by a German sniper, but many felt that a quick death by shooting was preferable to drowning in the

mud or being buried alive. And, as always, when it was time to be relieved
by the Worcesters on 6 December, came the horrendous slog back
down the long trench to Coigneux, with clothing and equipment made
'so heavy with wet mud'. The rain had been non-stop for that entire
period in the line, and they arrived 'drenched through but light hearted
at getting away from the trenches'.

They spent the 'rest period' in much the same way as before, digging
trenches and carrying out fatigues. Jack was detailed as company orderly
corporal, so was able to avoid much of the hard labour through carrying out his administrative duties. His platoon was billeted in an old barn,
which they inevitably shared with a sizeable colony of rats, but help was
at hand; Lidsey 'found a little French dog ratting in the garden at the back
of the house. We brought him in and put him in the loft over our barn;
had some real good sport – he killed ten in about three quarters of an
hour.' The fun was not to last, though – on 14 December, the battalion
went back to the trenches.

The following day, Wednesday 15th, the Germans decided to break
their quiet spell:

> During the night, the Bosches tried a bomb attack; our patrol
> discovered them before they got within throwing range and they
> were immediately enfiladed on both sides by machine guns. Only
> four bombs were thrown, doing no damage. The Germans left one
> dead man behind them; we could see where they had dragged several
> more, either killed or wounded, back to their lines. We brought the
> dead man in and gave him a respectable burial, the same procedure
> being gone through as if he was one of our own men. He had on
> him a solid gold Albert[61] and a pair of gold-rimmed spectacles; fire
> bombs; 30 rounds of ammunition; and a brand-new rifle.

Later, a British artillery barrage prompted a response from the Germans,
but many of their shells failed to go off. When the duds were examined,
they were 'found to contain burnt sawdust in place of explosives; they
had evidently been made by prisoners of war or Belgians'.

The foul weather of that winter continued. On the 16th, it 'rained all
night', leaving Jack 'very cold and miserable'. At 5.00 a.m. the next

morning, they were making their way to the fire trench when one of the platoon's junior NCOs, Corporal Webb, was taken ill, so Lidsey was ordered to take charge of Webb's section. The overnight rain had not let up, and it continued to pour down all day. Standing in a 'rotten' section of the trench known as D Sap for the next twelve hours, Jack described the trench as resembling a 'young river'.

Lidsey found himself in charge of his section in the fire trench on the night of the 20th, a still and moonlit night. Every now and again they could see and hear the Germans working on their own trenches, presumably having the same difficulties as the British in the saturated earth: 'One German shouted over that he was fed up with the war and that he wanted to get back as he had a wife and seven children in London! One of my fellows shouted back "if you don't keep your head down you'll have a widow and seven children". The German began shouting again but a few shots from my sentry soon quietened him down.'

As luck would have it, the Oxfordshires were out of the line for Christmas, leaving for Courcelles on 22 December. It was a tricky relief as their replacements, from the Worcestershire Regiment, were late, meaning that they had to move in daylight and thereby attracted 'live-liness' on their way out, but fortunately no one was hit. Christmas Eve was celebrated with a trip to the fumigator, followed by Jack bumping into an old friend from Magdalen College School named Roy Batten, now a sergeant in the Royal Engineers. The pair spent several hours catching up before Lidsey made his way to nearby Sailly where his section had been detailed to guard the bomb store, only to discover that in his absence they had 'done justice to eight bottles of Champagne'. Being the only sober one among them, Jack had to stand sentry alone for the next four hours, in case the orderly officer came around to inspect the guard, until his comrades 'got over it a bit'. The second Christmas of the war heralded further revelry that night:

Whilst on sentry another merry crew came round with biscuit tins for drums, tin whistles and flutes. They were about 20 officers from the Bombing School and the Sussex Regiment. They had also been celebrating Christmas, marching around Sailly kicking up Hell's delight and singing carols until 2am. When the officers got back to their billet, they were drinking neat whisky out of the bottle; one of them was brought back to the billet in a GS Wagon[62] and had to be carried up to bed; several of the others required assistance up the stairs.

His night of guarding detail finished, Jack returned to Courcelles on Christmas Day, where the battalion spent the day happily exempt from all fatigues. A six-a-side football tournament was organised, with the machine-gun section running out eventual winners against the team from Lidsey's C Company. Peace and goodwill were not on the agenda for everyone, though, as the Germans sent 'about 300 shells' into Sailly, which Jack had just left, in the afternoon, probably in response to British artillery who had been 'firing on their billets regularly every ten minutes for the last three or four days. Unfortunately one of the German shells found its mark, It crashed through the roof and table of the Artillery mess, just as they were cutting up their Christmas pudding. Two men were killed and several wounded. We spent the evening very quietly'. Boxing Day was celebrated in literal fashion, with Lidsey going 'a few rounds with the gloves'. He was knocked out and did the same to one of his comrades.

  With the seasonal festivities over, G Sector beckoned again, and they were back in the trenches on the 28th, two days sooner than expected. That night Jack was one of a party detailed to repair the barbed wire in front of their trench; the enemy knew that they were there and 'kept putting up lights and firing with machine-guns and rifles'. That same night, Lieutenant Philip Doyne of A Company went missing when he and another man went out to inspect the wire. A rescue party brought in his body two hours later, riddled with bullets from a German machine gun. The enemy was livelier this time than previously, with artillery, snipers and machine guns active daily. The unfortunate A Company bore the brunt of the hostility, losing a further four men killed by the end of the year.

  On the 30th, Lidsey was summoned to an interview with the brigade commander, Brigadier General James, regarding his commission application. James was 'pleased to sign' Jack's papers, and with that he had cleared the final administrative hurdle to becoming an officer. At some point in the near future, he would go off for training. Despite his elation however, 1915 ended on a very sour note:

Friday December 31st
Our artillery bombarded the Bosches heavily to knock the Old Year out. The Germans replied with whiz-bangs and had a lucky shot, hitting one of our sentry posts killing three men and wounding three. Our Platoon volunteered to bring the dead and wounded back to the village. We started immediately after dark, 4.30pm. We had to bring the bodies over a mile of very bad ground, all mud and shell holes every yard or two. Kept falling into shell holes and slipping down. When we were getting the men out of the trench, which was only 50 yards from the Germans, they heard us and turned three machine-guns on us and sent six whiz-bangs across; it was an absolute miracle that none of us were hit.

I think this was the hardest and most beastly job that I have ever had to do. We had to keep stopping to pick up the man's arm which kept falling off the stretcher. Got back around 10pm, wet through and smothered with mud and blood. We were all absolutely fagged out; the man my party carried weighed about 15 stone. If ever anyone deserved or earned a DCM,[63] the men that did this work did.

The New Year was ushered in with an artillery bombardment by both sides, with the Germans getting theirs in first since German time was one hour ahead of British time. The British barrage, however, 'included rockets and flares and was more artistic'.[64] By the time that this latest spell in the trenches came to an end on 3 January 1916, the Oxfordshires had taken twenty casualties, either killed or wounded. Of course, they made their weary way back to Coigneux – Jack observed ruefully that 'when I die, "Coigneux" will be on my dying breath'.

The Oxfords moved back into G Sector for the final time – at least for the time being – on the 9th. Again, the enemy was active, sending rifle grenades and shells over to welcome them back. The bombardment began at 2.00 p.m. and carried on until dusk, with shells landing 'at the rate of about 15 per minute'. The trenches were in their usual abysmal state, 'mud over the tops of our boots which stank perfectly awful. It gave me the

stomach ache from when we went in until we came out', Lidsey noted.
But the stench was probably preferable to the sustained mortar attack
the Germans subjected him to on the 11th:

> They strafed us very heavily with what we at first thought was a
> spring gun, but which we have found out is a 4" trench mortar.
> Nearly all day it was a very hot corner just around my post;
> fortunately, no-one was hit. I have never seen such awful
> expressions of fright on men's faces before, not even under the
> heaviest shelling that we've had. We simply stood and watched them
> come toppling over, apparently straight for us; they seemed to
> fascinate one as they came over. They exploded like a 5" shell
> (Howitzer). We were relieved at 5.30pm and jolly glad we were
> to get away too.

They moved back to the rear on the 15th to clean themselves up and
rest. The mobile bath unit at Sailly had taken delivery of a 'new system
of shower baths', which apparently delivered a 'very good bath indeed'.
So good, that Lidsey went bathing two days running, despite the Germans
attempting to disrupt his ablutions with an air raid. The battalion
remained in the Sailly and Coigneux area until 21 January, when they
took over trenches in K Sector facing Gommecourt Wood, a little north
of their old stretch in G Sector, from their local comrades of the
Buckinghamshire Battalion. The new trenches were 'an absolute paradise'
in comparison, with brick floors and hardly any water due to being on
higher ground. Furthermore, the communication trenches leading into
the front line were much shorter, making the journey in far easier. The
enemy was not about to make the stay a complete joy, however; on the
24th a section of the trench that Jack was in was blown in by a sudden
barrage of high-explosive shells that they then had to repair. That
night, his platoon was 'sent out on a patrol to Z Hedge, a hedge out
between the lines about 400 yards from our trenches and about 300 from
the German trench. We were out four hours; did not meet any Germans.
Found several 7ft lathes stuck upright in the ground with a bell on the
top. We had sense enough not to ring the bell or I have no doubt that
we should have had our money back (or something else).'

At 2.00 a.m. the following morning, Lidsey was woken by heavy shelling to the battalion's left, where the Warwickshires held the line: 'Our artillery replied very vigorously, It was a sight, everything was lit up as plain as day by the flashes from the exploding shells. The noise was terrific, one tremendous thundering roar. The Germans launched a bomb attack on the Warwicks on our left, under the cover of the artillery fire and 'Minenwerfers'. They got into the trench, killed two and wounded five Warwicks and took a Lewis Gun and 6 rifles.'

After that, though, the first trip into K Sector was relatively quiet, aside from several gas alarms, all of which turned out to be false. The Oxfords went back to Courcelles and Coigneux on the 27th, having taken no casualties. Their rest period was to last six days before being sent to K Sector again, with the unwelcome news that they were to stay in the line for the next thirty days. Even with better trenches, the prospect of being there for an extended period was distinctly unappealing, especially since the German front line was just '30 yards from ours'. Added to that, the nights were very cold, with temperatures down to ten degrees Fahrenheit, around minus twelve Centigrade. But again the enemy was fairly quiet, leading the Oxfordshires to believe they were facing new and inexperienced, or perhaps second-rate, German troops.

For Jack, though, the stay in the trenches was to be somewhat shorter than the month they had been told to expect. The news that he had been hoping for came through on Tuesday 8 February 1916, when his papers arrived 'for Blighty and commission', and he was ordered to pack up and be off at 10.00 a.m. the following morning. His journey was not made easy by the enemy, who sent him on his way with a heavy artillery barrage; he 'got out of the village in some hurry' and was 'never more pleased to leave Hébuterne than I was then; it was a really hot corner'. Lidsey made his way – along with another Ox & Bucks officer candidate, Private James Eldridge – to Louvencourt from where they would catch a train to Boulogne on the 10th. They were given a billet in a building officially named as the 'Leave Barn' but known to the troops as the 'Flea House' or the 'Lice House'. Not enamoured with the prospect of a night being bitten by vermin, they managed instead to find a double bed in a house normally reserved for officers going home on leave. That evening, the pair had dinner with the landlord and his family. Lidsey remarked:

I have never had such a funny dinner in my life:

1st Course: Soup; i.e. water that bacon had been boiled in

2nd Course: A little bit of fat boiled bacon, and some potatoes that had been mashed together

3rd Course: Salad resembling plantains and pork pie without any crust

4th Course: Coffee and bread and butter

Beer and bread with every course.

Next afternoon, Lidsey and Eldridge caught the train to Amiens, and then another to Boulogne, arriving at 5.00 a.m. on 11 February for the boat home to England and the prospect of four months' training to become officers.

Chapter Five

Temporary Gentleman, February – May 1916

A new system for officer training was introduced in early 1916, and Jack Lidsey would have been one of the first men selected for it. Officer Cadet Battalions (OCB) – largely staffed by officers and NCOs who had been wounded at the front and were unfit for further service – were raised specifically to train soldiers who had served in the ranks, or those who had been in the Officer Training Corps (OTC) while at school or university, for a commission. Hitherto, officers had been drawn from the upper echelons of society and were therefore considered to be gentlemen by default, even if their soldiering skills left much to be desired. The general feeling was that, since an officer came from noble stock, then the common soldier, being from the working classes and therefore naturally deferential, would follow him without question. But the horrendous scale of attrition among junior officers in the war's early years, coupled with the rapidly expanding size of the Army, meant that producing sufficient numbers of men who could lead and command was vital, leading to increasing quantities of officers from middle- or working-class backgrounds with little or no familiarity of the upper levels of military social hierarchy.

The British Army's high command was not overly concerned about the quality of leadership that a man from the ranks might provide, since a prospective candidate had to be recommended by his commanding officer and would have had combat experience and probably leadership skills through being an NCO, but it did have a worry that the man's social attributes might not be up to scratch. To that end, many of the OCBs were established in Oxbridge colleges or stately homes to give the candidate a grounding in 'gentlemanly' behaviour and to prepare them for the social expectations of the officers' mess. Basic instructions in etiquette were given, as well as sage advice about the need to keep lady-friends out of sight, and to get drunk in private rather than in front of the men. There were even lessons on how to walk like an officer; one Oxbridge OCB instructor apparently told his cadets to walk 'as if the whole bloody street belongs to you'. That said, the Army was keen that these new officers should not pretend to be something that they were not and warned them against feigning interest in horsemanship or emulating 'public school behaviour' such as manners and accent.[65] The term 'Temporary Gentleman' was initially applied to any civilian who was commissioned for 'hostilities only' regardless of social status, but after the establishment of the OCBs, it became a disparaging label for those officers from backgrounds regarded as inferior to those of their regular counterparts.

Attitudes towards Temporary Gentlemen within the Army were mixed. From some of the other ranks' perspectives, their new officer was from a similar background and had probably recently served as one of them, so he had experienced, and therefore understood, the Tommy's lot; others, however, regarded them with scorn, believing that they felt themselves better than the rest of the men and were acting above their station. Further, they found that, since their new officer had once been a private soldier, it was far harder to pull the wool over his eyes. As far as regular officers were concerned, opinions of temporary officers were generally based on their combat experience and effectiveness as leaders, and even some more traditional officers admitted that their lack of social graces was compensated by their effectiveness in the field. The poet and author Robert Graves, himself a product of Charterhouse and the OTC (and later an instructor at an OCB), sums up this attitude in his autobiography *Good-bye to All That* when he says that 'though the quality of officers had deteriorated from the regimental point of view, their greater efficiency in action amply compensated for their deficiency in manners'. Siegfried Sassoon, a pre-war officer, felt that the term 'Temporary Gentleman' was 'disgusting', and in most accounts of the war, it is not used, most likely because there were so many of them. The myth that the majority of subalterns in the First World War were teenaged former public school-boys is just that – a myth.

Of course, there was not universal acceptance among career officers, and a large degree of snobbishness persisted. Many regulars from the upper social strata noted with alarm the 'marked influx of men into the general officer corps whose social occupations were not "pukka", and [who] would not have had a sniff of a Territorial, let alone a Regular, commission in 1914'[66]. One public school-educated regular officer remarked that, 'many of them came from the lower middle class and had no manners, including table manners, of any kind; when my roommate, a captain, said, "I always wash me before I shave me", I felt that the bottom of the barrel had been scraped for officer material'[67]. Even Sassoon's protégé Wilfred Owen referred to Temporary Gentlemen in his letters as 'glorified NCOs' and 'privates and sergeants in masquerade'. A good example of a stereotypical Temporary Gentleman can be found in R.C. Sherriff's wonderful play *Journey's End* in the character of Trotter; short, fat, constantly eating and from a lower social class, he is in stark contrast to Stanhope, the public-school-educated hero, although still a capable and brave officer. Sherriff was more than qualified to pass observation on the characters of Trotter and Stanhope as he was himself a Temporary Gentleman. Despite having attended a good grammar school, it did not have an OTC so Sherriff had to join the Army as a private, working his way up to a commission through service in the ranks and then through an OCB, a carbon-copy of Lidsey's Army career path.

The essence of the OCB was to provide a four-month crash course in what the career officer would have been taught at the regular officer training schools such as Sandhurst or Woolwich, and previously at public school. While military training was provided (such as anti-gas measures, field engineering, open warfare, military law, map reading and reconnaissance), the emphasis of the course was on 'developing leadership and the cultivation of initiative and self-confidence'[68]. In other words, learning to be a gentleman; someone who had a natural ability to lead and whom the inherently reverent other ranks would follow automatically. For those like Jack who had already served in the ranks at the front, life at an OCB could be relatively benign, as evidenced by one officer cadet, an experienced former sergeant named George Ashurst, who said that:

'The routine was simple and the parades very easy. The most severe penalty for doing wrong was RTU – Returned to Unit – which meant, of course, being sent back to one's regiment in France. Any man who could not behave like a gentleman and conform to the simple rules of the camp certainly deserved RTU.'[69]

By 1917 there were twenty-three OCBs housed in a variety of university colleges, stately homes and former barracks. From the time of their creation until December 1918, almost 108,000 men were granted temporary commissions after successfully completing an OCB course, around half of all the commissions awarded throughout the First World War. The majority, like Lidsey, came from the middle classes and had held professional positions in civilian life, but a War Office study conducted after the war found that some forty per cent were of working-class stock – dockers, blacksmiths, miners and trawlermen all held temporary commissions. In most cases, the Temporary Gentleman was only too aware that his new status was just as the title described, temporary, for the duration of the war only. Many of them found that, on demobilisation, they were also 'de-officered' and discovered that going back to a white-collar occupation where they took orders rather than gave them was a shock to the system. Others, particularly those from the working classes, who had no job to return to often found themselves penniless, since their former officer status barred them from unemployment benefits and the labour exchange (provided for all ex-rank and file soldiers) on the assumption that they had been commissioned and therefore must have 'private means'; while that was generally true for career officers, it was certainly not the case for Temporary Gentlemen.

At the end of the war, over twenty per cent of the British Army's active infantry battalions were commanded by Temporary Gentlemen who had reached the rank of lieutenant colonel, but once the conflict was over and the necessity for wartime-only commissions had gone, the Army went back to its class-based measure of what qualities made a good officer. Some temporary officers tried for regular commissions after the war but most were unsuccessful, and even those few who did manage to stay on found themselves susceptible to redundancy during the post-war austerity drive of the 1920s, the so-called 'Geddes Axe'. A few even went so far as to resign their commissions in order to stay in the Army, back in the ranks.

Jack Lidsey's name appeared in the *London Gazette* of 18 February 1916, recording that he was to be 'Second Lieutenant (on probation)' from 12 February, the day he arrived at his OCB. He did not keep a diary while he was in officer training, so we do not know to which OCB he was sent, or what he thought of the experience. He does mention in an entry after he went back to France following commissioning that the billet he was in was a 'paradise after Salisbury Plain', so we can deduce that at least some of his time was spent there. Wherever it was he went, and whatever he felt, he was successful, and so it was that, with his probation over upon graduation, he became a Temporary Gentleman. James Eldridge, his travelling companion from France, is listed alongside him in the *London Gazette*, also as a probationary second lieutenant, but his name does not appear in the roll of officers of the 1/4 (Oxfordshire) Battalion who took part in the First World War, so it is likely that he was posted to a different battalion or even regiment after the OCB (unless he failed the course and was 'RTUd'). For Jack, though, he was to be reunited with the Oxfordshires.

Chapter Six

The Somme, 29 May – 30 June 1916

Second Lieutenant William John Lidsey, along with seven other Ox & Bucks officers, sailed from Southampton at 8.15 p.m. on 29 May 1916 aboard the SS *Copenhagen*,[70] bound for France once more. The crossing was 'beautifully calm', and the ship docked at Le Havre at 4.30 a.m. the next morning, although the passengers were kept on board until 9.00 a.m. without being fed. Once finally allowed to disembark, Jack went into the town and breakfasted on strawberries and eggs, before reporting to 18 Camp, one of the many British Army rest and reception camps in the Le Havre area, where he was told to await transport orders for onward travel to the Oxfordshires. The 18 Camp officers' quarters were very good, boasting a garden with sweet peas and roses, and a vegetable patch; Jack's aforementioned 'paradise'. His orders were to leave Le Havre at midnight on the 31st, so he spent a leisurely day wandering about the town and eating until the time came to catch the train to Rouen. Arriving at 7.30 a.m., and with no train scheduled until early afternoon, Lidsey availed himself of the restaurant at the Hotel Moderne. Setting off again, he slept well on the train, even though it was a lengthy journey, finally arriving at Fienvillers station early on 2 June. From the station, he and his companions marched into the village, had breakfast, and then cadged a lift by lorry to Neuville before another march to Oneux, where they finally found the Oxfordshire Battalion. Their arrival was greeted with surprise – no one knew they were coming. Once the welcomes and introductions were done, the new arrivals were swiftly allocated to their various companies. Jack, along with Second Lieutenant J.G. Shepherd, went to

A Company; Hunt and Lay to B Company; Jefferson and Townsend to C Company; and Sherrington and Millard to D Company.

Reporting to the A Company CO, Captain F.B. Jones, Lidsey was given command of 3 Platoon, with between thirty and forty men in his charge. His first impression of his soldiers was 'very good'. For their part, the troops were probably pleased to have an experienced officer, albeit a newly appointed one, and someone already familiar to them.

Jack had arrived just in time to begin preparations for a major offensive, the Battle of the Somme. After the lack of movement against the Germans in 1915, the Allies had, at a conference held in Chantilly that December, agreed to a joint strategy for the coming year. A combined attack would suffocate the Germans and restrict their ability to move their reserves to wherever they were most needed. The French and British commanders, Joffre and Haig, met in February 1916 to flesh out their parts of the grand plan. They agreed to a combined offensive, with the French playing the major role and the British in support, in the summer of 1916, and the date was set for 1 July. The logical place for the assault was in the valley of the River Somme, the junction of the two Allied armies. The central idea of the plan was to cause the Germans more casualties than they could sustain, thereby forcing them to capitulate.

However, the enemy was to scupper the plan before it was set in motion. Just a week after the two Allied generals met, the Germans attacked the French at Verdun, similarly intending to cause disproportionate losses to the French Army. France could not now commit to the Somme offensive as the main partner, since Verdun was drawing its troops away from the Somme as reinforcements were needed to prevent a collapse there. With the situation becoming increasingly desperate, Joffre pleaded with Haig to attack to take some of the pressure off his beleaguered army. The British were now to take the lead on the Somme with the French in support – not what had been planned. The offensive was to be preceded by a massive, week-long artillery barrage designed to shred the German barbed wire and obliterate the enemy trenches and dugouts before the first wave of advancing British troops reached them. The die was now cast and the Oxfordshires, as part of the 48th (South Midland) Division, were to be involved.

The battalion began preparations for the attack in earnest with less than a month to go. On 4 June, the Oxfordshires moved to Agenvillers, about four miles away from Oneux. Here, they spent the next five days, mostly in rain, practising assaults in formations of various sizes from company level up to brigade proportions. Jack's twenty-first birthday came on the 6th, with no mention of it made in his diary – the intensity of training most likely had his attention focused elsewhere. Soon it was the Oxfords' turn to head for the line once more. Leaving Agenvillers at 4.00 a.m. on the 10th, they marched sixteen miles in frequent thunderstorms to Mézerolles, some twenty miles to the north-west of Albert. Jack's 3 Platoon brought up the very rear of the battalion column, sweeping up stragglers and slowing the traffic behind them for safety. He was pleased with their march, observing that not one of his platoon, or indeed of A Company as a whole, fell out of line. After a night on a hard, stone floor in a 'rotten' billet, and hearing of a German advance of six kilometres at Verdun, the battalion struck out again next morning for a fifteen-mile hike eastwards to Couin, arriving there with 'very sore feet' at around 4.00 p.m. This time they slept under canvas, a welcome development since it was raining and they had expected to spend the night in the open. They left for the trenches at 8.30 a.m. the following day, relieving the Royal Warwickshires in the familiar surroundings of G Sector at Hébuterne. Lidsey's platoon was sent to the reserve dugouts, where he mused, perhaps a little ruefully, that 'it was exactly four months today that I left Hébuterne for home; it does not seem so long. The old trenches seem much the same.'

The weather was awful for high summer. Continuous rain made conditions in the trenches miserable, despite the vain efforts of the troops to pump the water out. Still, Jack's dugout was reasonable, and the enemy, so far, had been relatively quiet. That was to change on 14 June when 3 Platoon went first into the support- and, later, the fire trenches. Canister bombs and rifle grenades rained down from the German trenches, fortunately causing no casualties. The strafing continued next day, with five direct hits on 3 Platoon's position, but again, Lidsey's men somehow escaped unscathed. That evening, the Germans raised the stakes with a heavy bombardment that was answered by the guns of the Royal Field Artillery peppering the enemy with shrapnel rounds, which 'quietened them immediately'.

At just after midnight that night, Lidsey and his men were on alert. The battalion next to them, the 7th Worcesters, were about to go on a trench raid to grab a prisoner. The Germans were suspected to be swapping out their front-line troops, and the British wanted to know who was coming in to face them. Slipping across no-man's-land under the cover of the darkness, the Worcesters encountered the enemy wire, which they intended to blow with Bangalore torpedoes.[71] The wire was so thick that the attack failed – the Bangalores made no path through it. As soon as the charges were blown, the Germans opened fire with machine guns, forcing the Worcesters back the way they had come, empty-handed. British artillery then began a covering barrage, bringing the night alive with gunfire, star shells and flares. For forty-five minutes, shrapnel and high-explosive shells poured down on the German trenches, but even with the gunners' help, the Worcesters took several casualties. It was a wasted, costly effort.

With the night's excitement over, the Oxfordshires were relieved by the Buckinghamshires the next afternoon. In reserve once more, it was by now obvious that the great attack was not far away, with guns and ammunition dumps appearing everywhere. The artillery was sending registration rounds towards enemy targets regularly, which made the Germans suspicious. Enemy aircraft were frequent visitors over the British lines, trying to work out what was afoot. For the next few days and nights, Jack and his men worked on improving the trenches and wire, as well as bringing up supplies for the impending assault. On the evening of 21 June, 3 Platoon went to Hébuterne to collect huge boxes of engineering equipment and deliver them to the front-line trenches. They had only made it halfway when they were stopped – British trench mortars were about to open up on the Germans, and a retaliatory barrage was expected in return. Sure enough, just after midnight, a short, sharp enemy shoot hit the British trenches, but luckily did no major damage. Resuming their heavy work, Lidsey saw large numbers of gas cylinders also being ferried to the front, and he overheard one man saying 'we've carried enough gas up tonight to gas the whole of the bloody German army ten times over!'.

The Oxfordshires moved back to Couin on 22 June, two miles further behind the lines. The pace and intensity of the work continued. Parties of men laboured all day, digging trenches to carry telephone cables; bringing up more and more engineering equipment; ferrying smoke bombs to the front line at night; stockpiling rations; and carrying out firing practice, sometimes wearing their cumbersome smoke hoods, on a makeshift range dug into a nearby hillside. A huge summer storm hit them the next day; they watched as the thunderheads built up in the late June afternoon heat, before the wind picked up and pushed the angry clouds their way.

Frantically, they dug storm drains around their tents just in time, but a nearby observation balloon wasn't so lucky. The dirigible's handlers were desperately trying to haul it down and had it only sixty feet from the ground when a strong gust caught it, jerking the cable tether taught before it parted with a snap, sending the balloon careering and bucking away into the sky and sailing over the German lines at a great rate of knots. Suddenly, the heavens opened, and nearly all the Oxford's bivouacs were torn to shreds and their kit drenched. The sound of thunder was continuous, so much so that Jack was sure that the artillery had opened fire for the 'big boost'. That evening, after the storm had abated and they had repaired their camp, he had a champagne dinner to belatedly celebrate his coming of age on the 6th.

Lidsey did not have to wait much longer for the pre-attack barrage to start. On 24 June, after another hefty storm the previous night, the guns began to bark at 9.00 a.m. The ferocity of the bombardment was unprecedented – the battles of Loos and Neuve Chapelle the year before had seen nothing like this. General Sir Henry Rawlinson, commander of the British Fourth Army, which would make the assault and of which the Oxfordshires was a part, had available to him over 800 18-pounder field guns; 32 4.7-inch guns; 128 60-pounder guns; 20 6-inch guns; 1 9.2-inch gun; 1 12-inch gun; 202 4.5-inch howitzers; 104 6-inch howitzers; 64 8-inch howitzers; 60 9.2-inch howitzers; 11 12-inch howitzers; 6 15-inch howitzers; 16 French 220mm howitzers; 60 French 75mm guns; and 24 French 120mm guns. In addition, there were 288 medium and 28 heavy trench mortars, as well as gas, smoke and flame-throwers. Available ammunition for all the guns totalled around 3,000,000[72] rounds. Rawlinson himself said that 'nothing could exist at the conclusion of the bombardment in the area covered by it', and given the amount of weaponry at his disposal, it is easy to see why he had so much confidence. There were almost twice as many guns (when viewed on a 'per yard of front' basis) in terms of heavy artillery, and a quarter more in field artillery, than had been deployed at the Battle of Loos in 1915.

The field artillery, the 18-pounders and the 4.5-inch howitzers, opened fire first to strip away the enemy's wire before the heavy guns joined in to smash his trenches and dugouts with their massive shells. Jack and his fellow officers were awestruck by the destructive power being unleashed around them and climbed a hill after dark to watch. Muzzle flashes lit the horizon for miles around, and the noise never ceased. It was, Lidsey said, 'a wonderful sight'.

The weather cleared the next day, bringing German aircraft over to spot targets for their own guns in an attempt to retaliate for the British onslaught. Around a dozen enemy machines ventured over the front around the Oxfordshires, but these 'were soon driven back'. Three 'Hun' observation balloons were brought down by the Royal Flying Corps, keeping their prying eyes away from the build-up. Being a Sunday, Jack went with the other Oxfordshires to communion, where the padre 'cheered us all up by telling us that it was probably the last we should ever have'. It was certainly not what the men wanted to hear.

With German counter-artillery fire reaching them sporadically, the Oxfords struck camp on the 26th and moved to the far side of Couin where their new pitches weren't so easily seen by the enemy. The site was also freer-draining, and so slightly drier, which was welcome since the heavy downpours continued. The first gas of the preparatory attack was released by the British on the Oxfordshire's right; Jack observed that 'they [the Germans] got the wind up terribly and shelled the front line very heavily'.

The day of the 'big boost' edged ever closer, and the guns never stopped firing. On 27 June, A Company of the Oxfordshires paraded for inspection in fighting order by the commander of 145 Brigade. Each man carried his Short Magazine Lee-Enfield rifle with 150 rounds of ammunition in webbing pouches; his smoke hood in its haversack; small pack (on his back) containing emergency rations, mess tins, spare socks, groundsheet, basic wash and shave kit and some personal possessions; two-pint water bottle; entrenching tool; bayonet; and his 'Brodie' steel

helmet on his head. In all, the troops each hefted around 65lb of equipment, while some had extra ammunition in bandoliers, hand grenades,
wire cutters and other battlefield paraphernalia, all adding to the load.
Once the parade was over and the brigadier pronounced himself satisfied,
the Oxfordshires released some of the nervous tension that had been
building up over the previous days by swimming in the nearby river ('very
cold – did not stay in more than a minute'), and holding a sports day:
'Very good fun, races including bombing competitions, tug-of-war, relay
races, obstacle races (putting on equipment and gas helmets and running
100 yards)[73], sergeants' 100 yards handicap and officers ditto; arrived
equal third, starting from scratch – the other three had 10 yards start.[74]
Prizes were given; complete success; men very pleased.'

The prudence of moving camp the day before was amply demonstrated
when half a dozen German artillery rounds fell on their old campsite;
it had been a lucky escape.

Thursday 29 June dawned a little brighter than the previous couple
of rain-swept days. Jack Lidsey began his day with two and a half hours
of physical exercise and bayonet practice with 3 Platoon, honing their
skills and condition still further for the coming attack. He had just
dismissed his men and was about to go and find some lunch when he
was summoned to see the battalion CO, Lieutenant Colonel Bartlett.
Sensing that something was afoot, Jack arrived at Battalion HQ to find
that his friend, Second Lieutenant Tom Fortescue, and another officer,
Second Lieutenant S. Smith, were waiting for him. Bartlett explained that
the 'big boost' was now just days away, and that accurate intelligence was
needed about the state of the German wire and trenches in front of them,
and what effect the bombardment was having on the enemy's morale.
There was only one way to gather the information, and that was at first
hand. He gave orders that a raid was to be carried out on the trenches
opposite, with the aim of bringing back a prisoner for interrogation.
Fortescue was to command the raiding party, backed by Lidsey and Smith
who would lead two groups of fifty men each. Bartlett impressed upon
them the vital importance of the mission – the success of the assault in
their area could well depend on what the captives had to say. They were
to go the next night.

Fortescue, Smith and Lidsey made their way back to their tents to formulate their plan of action. It was a thankless task – trench raids were notoriously dangerous undertakings since the enemy was always alert to there possibility; they had already seen what had happened when the Worcesters had tried a raid a couple of weeks earlier. Getting out of the fire trench, across no-man's-land, through the enemy wire into the German trench, apprehending an unwilling 'Hun' or two, and then getting everyone back safely would be no mean feat. Still, someone had to it, and it was they who had been selected.

The success or otherwise of the raid was going to depend in no small part on the state of the German barbed wire. If it had been cut by the artillery, then getting into, and out of, the enemy trench swiftly would be that much easier. Fortescue and Lidsey decided to take a couple of horses and ride to see the gunnery officer who had been barraging the wire to see what he thought. Smith stayed behind to begin putting the detail into the raid plan. The artillery batteries were positioned around the village of Sailly-au-Bois, around three miles west of Couin. Jack and Fortescue searched for almost an hour before they managed to track the field artillery colonel down; he told them to go and speak to the forward observation officer (FOO) at the observation post (OP) from where the wire-cutting shoot was being directed. The OP was close to the front line, and the noise and flash of the guns was tremendous, unsettling the horses. Leaving their mounts behind a hay rick some way back, the pair decided to walk the last leg from Hébuterne to the OP. Down in the dimly lit dugout, the FOO did not offer much in the way of encouragement, telling the two infantry officers that it was impossible to cut the wire as his guns were too far away from the target, on the limit of their range. He had already put some 4,000 rounds of 18-pounder ammunition on to the wire, but with little effect. This was not good news.

Fortescue decided that they should take a look at the ground, and reconnoitre their start point. Making their way to the fire trench from where they would pull their 'stunt', they could scarcely believe their eyes when they got there. The trench was 'in a very bad state, all knocked in and no attempt had been made to clean it (as is usual with the Warwicks); just where we wanted to leave the trench there were 3,000 sulphur bombs, all detonated [primed]. Had a good look round and took our directions by compass bearings.'

Fuming about the state of the trench, they went to seek out the CO of the Warwicks to complain. There was no way they could use it as it was, half-collapsed and with a huge stack of lethal sulphur grenades in the way – it was a disaster waiting to happen, especially as they would be moving off in the dark. The Warwick's colonel promised to have the grenades moved out of the trench, and to do what he could to shore up the walls.

Returning to where they had secured their horses, Lidsey and Fortescue made their way back to Couin, ruminating on what they had discovered and exchanging views. Arriving back at 6.30 p.m., they discussed the plan that Smith had been working on. He recommended that the raiding party be halved in size – 100 men was far too large a body to control effectively in the dark, and to have any hope of keeping quiet to preserve the element of surprise that they needed. A second party with two Lewis Guns and twenty-five men could then remain behind in the fire trench to give covering fire should it be needed. Fortescue agreed; fifty men stood a better chance of success.

Jack realised that he was hungry. He had eaten nothing since breakfast, so he managed to seize half an hour to grab a bite to eat before the trio briefed the plan to the CO. Bartlett listened carefully, making the odd observation and asking a few questions. He approved the recommendation of a smaller group, trusting the judgement of his junior officers. Satisfied that everything had been covered and all the necessary arrangements had been made, Bartlett shook the three men's hands in turn and wished them good luck, reminding them, as if they needed it, of the importance of their mission. He, and the rest of the brigade, were depending on them.

Gathering the men who were to take part in the raid, Fortescue, Lidsey and Smith led the party out of the Couin camp at 7.30 p.m. to the local church, where they were pleasantly surprised to find that motor transport had been laid on to take them as far as Sailly – not quite so much foot-slogging that night. A short march then took them up to Hébuterne where they fell the men out to prepare for the raid before they went into the fire trench, their jumping-off point. Tea was brewed, and bread and cheese were produced from somewhere. Equipment, such as it was, was checked and rechecked – the men carried the bare minimum to aid swift movement. Many of the troops had left their noisy and cumbersome rifles behind in favour of clubs, knives, entrenching tools and knuckledusters – trench raiding was a silent, medieval sport. Soot from burned corks was rubbed into the men's faces and hands, and the fine detail of the plan was gone over once more. There was nothing else to do now but wait for darkness.

Just after midnight, Fortescue gave the order to move into the fire trench. Progressing as silently as they could, they edged into the narrow space. Hearing a murmured curse from the front, Jack pushed his way past the men to see what was wrong. Fortescue pointed – the live sulphur bombs were still there. Enraged, Lidsey went back to the support trench they had just passed through and grabbed one of the Warwickshires' junior officers: 'I swore at him as hard as I could; positively lost my temper. It frightened him to death; he cleared off like lightning with his tail between his legs.'

There was no time now to wait for the bombs to be cleared; the Oxfordshires would just have to manage as best they could. With his watch telling him that it was time to go, Jack eased himself over the lip of the trench parapet, his stomach pressed to the ground. Pausing to listen, he signalled for his group of raiders to follow, inching himself forwards to make way for them behind him. Checking that they were all with him, he then set about carefully cutting a gap in their own wire, an opening that they would have to find in the dark on their way back.

Painstakingly, they cleared enough of the wire to get through – the way to the enemy was now open. Jack glanced left and right trying to fix a picture of the gap in the wire in his mind for when they returned, and then gestured his men to follow him. Inching forward across no-man's-land and using shell craters for cover, they crawled ever closer to the German trenches. They could hear mumbled voices and smell the cigarette smoke that curled its way towards them on the night breeze.

Probing gently in front of him in the dark, Lidsey's fingers touched something cold and sharp; they had reached the first line of enemy barbed wire. So far, so good. The wire had been breached in several places, just needing a snip with the cutters here and there to help them through. One by one the raiders crawled through the gaps, knowing that this line of wire would not be the last. Making certain once again that he had all his men, Lidsey resumed his slow progress forward. After what seemed an eternity, they reached the second barbed-wire line, just twenty-five yards in front of the German parapet, only to discover that the gunner FOO back in Hébuterne had been absolutely right – this wire, being further away from his guns, was intact and completely untouched by the thousands of 18-pounder shells thrown at it. The concertina wire was at least eight coils deep, held upright by iron corkscrew stakes – it was impassable.

Jack hesitated in the dark, considering what to do next. Before he had come to a decision, the night exploded around him. Shouts of alarm from the German trench just in front of him were followed by a shower of stick grenades cartwheeling through the nocturnal air. Retreating into no-man's-land, he decided to move the group a little to the right and try to find a way through the wire there, but it was no good; the 'Huns' spotted them and sent more grenades looping in their direction. The raiders shifted left, past where they had first met the intact wire, but again they were seen. Illumination flares were bursting over their heads now, blanching the ground with white light and exposing them to the enemy. More grenades, now joined by volleys of rifle fire. All pretence of surprise was lost; the British troops could only press themselves into the mud and try to be as inconspicuous as possible. The German artillery opened fire, dropping 'whiz-bangs', the 'Hun' equivalent of the British eighteen-pounder round, into no-man's-land to winkle the raiders out. Jack and his men laid low – 'I have never laid so close to the ground before.' There was no alternative; they could not go forward through the wire, so the only thing to do was to go back to their own lines. One man took a bullet in the cheek but survived, and one of the NCOs, who had decided to bring his rifle with him, had the weapon's butt smashed by a bullet. Lidsey himself was extremely lucky as 'a bullet rung my shrapnel helmet like a bell'.

Two hours after setting out, the group flung themselves back into the relative safety of their fire trench. Casualties had been mercifully light, but the objective of the raid had failed – they had no prisoner to show for their efforts. The battalion War Diary recorded that 'the whole party retired in excellent order, and although the main objective of the expedition had not been attained, the whole affair was very creditably conducted'.[75] Lieutenant Colonel Bartlett declared himself happy with the information they had been able to bring back about the condition of the wire. If it was the same story along the entire fourteen-mile front of Fourth Army's looming attack, then it would be a disaster. To round off the misery of the night, it poured with rain on the march back to Couin, with no transport for them this time. Jack flopped, exhausted, into his bivouac at 6.30 a.m. on 30 June. His uniform had been torn on the enemy wire, and he was stiff with fatigue. When he woke later that day, the artillery bombardment was still raging, perhaps with even greater intensity. Some said that the rumble of the guns could be heard on Hampstead Heath back in London. Lidsey noted that 'the Hun must be having a rough time'. That was nothing compared to the experience that Rawlinson's Fourth Army was to have the following day.

Chapter Seven

The Somme, 1 July – 31 August 1916

Saturday 1 July 1916 broke hot and sunny, a perfect summer's day. For the British assault troops, crammed into the fire trenches, it was to prove a day from hell. As the whistles blew along the line at 7.30 a.m. and the first attacking waves clambered up their ladders and out into no-man's-land, it was soon all too horribly obvious that the reliance on the effectiveness of the artillery barrage had been misplaced. In some locations the enemy wire had indeed been broken, but for the most part it had survived intact, as Jack had discovered the previous night. The intended effect of the shelling had not been properly understood, and instead of being shredded as predicted, the coils of wire had simply been blown up into the air by the explosions and then dropped straight back down to where they had been before, like 'slinky' springs picked up and discarded by a child. As for the German dugouts, they were far too deep underground to have been destroyed, even by the heavy shells of the howitzers. The 'Huns' had taken refuge beneath the earth until the barrage stopped – a clear sign that the British would soon be advancing – and then emerged from their shelters up into the trenches and set up their machine guns. Of the almost 2,000,000 shells fired by British artillery in the pre-attack barrage, many were duds and failed to explode. The manufacture and supply of ammunition had been a case of quantity over quality.

Many of the British Fourth Army troops that day were the men of Kitchener's New Army, those who had volunteered at the outbreak of war as their patriotic duty. They had been waiting for their chance for almost two years; they were keen and well trained, but largely untried in battle. Told to walk across no-man's-land because there would be no opposition to meet them and no wire to stop them, the soldiers of the so-called Pals battalions were cut to pieces.

On the extreme left, or north, of the Fourth Army's attack was VIII Corps, with the 48th (South Midland) Division, containing the 1/4 Battalion Oxfordshire & Buckinghamshire Light Infantry, holding the corp's left flank. At 8.30 a.m., the Oxfordshires struck camp at Couin and marched to the village of Mailly-Maillet, just west of Beaumont-Hamel, which was an objective for the first day. The initial rumours were already beginning to filter back from the 'big boost', and Jack recorded that 'things were going well'. Resting at Mailly-Maillet, the men dumped their excess kit and got into fighting order, ready to go into action if needed. By 4.30 p.m., Lidsey heard that the left and centre divisions of VIII Corps had 'gained their objectives and the right Div, to which we are in support, was held up behind Beaumont-Hamel but is now pushing on and has nearly reached its objective. Later news – Serre and Miraumont have been taken.'

The rumours were all quite untrue. The 31st Division, a New Army division of Pals battalions, had left its trenches in front of Serre and advanced up the slope towards the fortified village. Although a small group of men did manage to reach the village, most were beaten back as soon as they left the fire trenches. The Accrington Pals, for example, lost 235 killed and 350 wounded out of 700 who started the attack, all within the first 20 minutes and 100 yards of where they had begun. A German counter-attack later threw out those few British troops in Serre itself. At Beaumont-Hamel the story was much the same: the 4th and 29th Divisions were scythed down by German machine-gunners, with the Newfoundland Regiment, part of the 29th Division, taking ninety-one per cent casualties for no gain. As for Miraumont, the British never got anywhere near the village that day and still had not taken it the following November when the Somme campaign was over. Although gains had been made in the southern area of the attack, it was a different story in the northern sector. As the day finished, the casualty figures across the Fourth Army made for truly shocking reading – over 57,000 dead, missing, wounded or taken prisoner. It was, and still is, the bloodiest day in the entire history of the British Army.

The South Midland Division was held in reserve on 1 July, meaning that Lidsey and his men were saved from the slaughter of the opening moves. As the new dawn arrived, the news was less optimistic. Jack heard that a strong German counter-attack had 'driven us back into our original line all along the Corps front'. Battalion HQ received a bulletin that summed up the previous day well: 'French on the Somme and the southern Corps of Fourth Army have made good progress; the northern Corps of Fourth Army, including VIII Corps, have made no progress.'[76]

Orders came down from brigade at 9.30 a.m. that the Oxfordshires were to prepare to attack the next morning, on 3 July. Their objective was to capture and hold three lines of German trenches just to the north of the Ancre River near Beaumont-Hamel, not far from where the Newfoundlanders had been decimated the day before. The scheme of attack was passed down to the company commanders, who broke the orders down further for each platoon. Jack gave his men their instructions and got them into fighting order before they moved off to the village of Mesnil at 8.00 p.m., from where they waited in a sunken lane to be sent into battle. The tension began to mount; this was far worse than a trench raid – this was to be a concerted attack against a determined enemy. The worst thing was the waiting, and they just wanted to get it over with. At 1.00 a.m. the order came – the attack was cancelled. Lidsey recorded his frustration, stating that 'everyone very downhearted as our blood was up; so terribly keen on not having another winter out here'.

Deflated, they trudged back to Mailly-Maillet, where they met the 'remains of a regiment' from the previous day's attack. These lucky survivors were sporting the souvenirs of war, particularly the prized 'Pickelhaube' – the spiked German helmet. The Oxfordshires vowed that, when it was their turn, they would 'have one each'. Later that day they were ordered back to Couin, a march completed in stifling heat and dust. Arriving there at 8.30 p.m., there was little else to do than turn in for an early night.

The heavens opened the next day, damping down the dust and cooling everyone off. That afternoon the battalion was sent back into the trenches at its old stamping ground of G Sector at Hébuterne. The march-in was made in hot sun, interspersed with frequent torrential downpours along the way. It was a long evening and night since, before they could move, all the fighting equipment that had been issued for the cancelled attack had to be collected in, meaning a delay in setting off. Then, on arrival, they found that the Warwickshires, whom they were to replace, were dispersed differently to the Oxfordshires' plan, so everyone had to be shuffled around. It was midnight before each man was finally in the right place. The support trenches were in no better condition than the last time they were in them, not helped by the flash floods that the summer storms had brought, and the mud was above the knees in places. Jack managed to share a reasonable dugout with an officer from the Machine-gun Company, which had a 'very nice and comfortable wire bed'.

Wednesday 5 July heralded better weather. Sun and a warm wind helped to dry out the stinking trenches, aided by Jack's men pumping the water out with hand pumps. The clean-up took all day, but by early evening they had managed to 'get it quite respectably clean'. All day long the British artillery kept up its barrage with the object of keeping open what gaps in the enemy wire it had succeeded in forcing, and ceaseless machine-gun fire also poured towards the German trenches to keep their opponents' heads down. However, A Company took its first casualties of the Somme battle that day when Private J. Telfer was killed by return fire, and another man standing with him was wounded. Three more men were hit while bringing up rations from the village to the trenches.

If Lidsey felt that the support trenches were in a bad way, then he had a rude awakening when they moved up to the fire trenches that evening. They were 'in an awful state', worse than they were the previous winter, with water and mud well over knee height throughout. There was nothing for it but to toil throughout the night with the hand pumps once more.

As the short summer night gave way to the breaking day, Jack peered out over the parapet into no-man's-land and was horrified by the sight that greeted him:

Daylight revealed the awful scene in front of, and in, the trenches on our right, from which the 29th Div attacked. About two hundred

dead between the lines. During the day a man crawled in that had
been out there since Sunday morning. He had a shattered knee and
a broken arm. He was in fine spirits; he had lived on grass and water
from shell holes. He said that 4 others had started in with him this
morning; nothing has been seen of them. The smell begins to
get awful.

To keep their minds from the carnage in front of them, Lidsey's men
busied themselves with clearing out the muck and filth from the trenches.
As the sun rose higher, bringing another hot day, the stench from the
corpses soon became overpowering, and the Oxfords were more than
happy when they were relieved at 10.00 p.m. and were able to leave the
front line behind them. When they got back to their bivouacs at Sailly-
au-Bois, Lidsey carried out a foot inspection of his platoon. As he had
suspected, trench foot was becoming a problem, and everyone's feet were
'very bad indeed'; certainly not what was expected during the suppos-
edly dry summer months. The rain returned the next morning and
carried on well into the late afternoon, and the trenches that they had
worked so hard to clear simply filled up with water and mud again.
Thankful that, for a few days at least, they did not have to go back into
the line, Lidsey and his men tried to get what rest they could, an almost
impossible task in the pouring rain: 'Had difficulty in finding a dry place
to sleep in. When we lay down on our ground sheets, the ground was
so soft we sank right in. Rained hard until 11pm and part of the night
as well.'

   They set about trying to improve their lot, 'erecting a very elaborate
tent from ground sheets for our (A Company) Mess and living room;
the result was highly successful'. The rain eventually stopped and the
wind picked up, and the wet began, slowly, to dry out. Aside from making
their own lives better, they were detailed with working parties, taking
supplies and rations up to the front line. On the 8th, Lidsey led a group
of eighty men up the line to carry gas cylinders back to the rear – it was
arduous work because of the state of the trenches, and the fact that the
Germans were shelling them with 'whiz-bangs' as they went. One of Jack's
sergeants was hit in the shoulder, and a corporal was evacuated with
concussion. Shouldering one of the heavy cylinders himself, Jack

stumbled through the quagmire, constantly ducking when the scream of an enemy shell was heard. He was 'jolly glad when we had finished'. Smothered with mud, he eventually made it back to his bivouac at 3.00 a.m. the next morning. Taking advantage of a no-work period, he slept throughout the day.

He missed a huge task for the battalion on 10 July, when those not on rest were ordered to join the remainder of the brigade in 'advancing the front line 500 yards between the Puisieux and Serre roads'[77]. Six hundred of the Oxfordshires went up to help dig a new trench system towards the Germans, who of course were not about to let the British work unhindered. A mixture of trench mortars and artillery rounds were sent towards the new trench as the men laboured to complete it, which they did in record time – about two hours. The work was not without cost: the Oxfordshires lost three men killed and several others wounded.

It was their turn in the front line at G Sector once more. Moving up on 12 July, A Company took its position in the right fire trench, known as Worcester Street, no doubt named by its former occupants. Work to strengthen the trench and its defences was continuous and extremely hazardous – they 'put up 100 yards of wire entanglements in record time, under fire of Minenwerfers,[78] whiz-bangs, and more especially machine-guns. Had no casualties; was knocked down by the concussion from a "Minnie"; my bugler was thrown onto a heap of shovels.'

The strain of being in the front line was beginning to tell. Private C. Rouse was sentenced that day to ten years' penal servitude by court martial for refusing to go on patrol when ordered to do so on the night of 6–7 July.[79] That he was tried and convicted so soon after his crime speaks volumes about the need for military justice to be not only a punishment but a deterrent for the other men, particularly during a major offensive.

Lidsey had been working for twenty-four hours when he was finally able to get some rest at 3.00 a.m. the next morning. He emerged from his dugout a few hours later to do his morning inspection rounds and was surprised to find that 'a few thousand' smoke bombs had been delivered to the trench in the small hours to 'fumigate the Hun as soon as the wind is favourable'. He shook his head in disbelief: 'no doubt he [the 'Hun'] laughs at us. The joke is getting too stale. He must think us bloody fools'. A Company was replaced by C Company at 10.00 p.m. that night, and an hour later the Germans welcomed the new arrivals with a thirty-minute artillery barrage.

The smoke bombs Jack had seen were put to use the next day. With the breeze blowing towards the enemy trenches, smoke and gas were released along the entire 48th Division front for around an hour at dawn. The intention was to fool the Germans into thinking that an attack was coming in the northern area of the Somme battlefront as a diversion from the genuine assault on the German second-line positions to the south. To compound the deception, the British troops in the north were ordered to show fixed bayonets above the parapet, and the Lewis Gunners kept up a constant hail of fire towards the enemy. The Germans presumably swallowed the bait as they responded furiously with artillery and machine-gun fire for the next two hours. The attack in the south marked the opening of the second phase of the Somme operation, the Battle of Bazentin Ridge. As the news of the fresh assault came through to the Oxfordshires that evening, there was a sense of optimism; Bazentin-le-Grand and Bazentin-le-Petit had apparently fallen, with Indian cavalry leading the way through the enemy lines. Lidsey wrote, excitedly: 'We are very cheery and expect to be moved down to Contalmaison to chase the Hun; we are looking forward eagerly to getting away from this part of the line. Don't mind what we do if we can get away from here. We are absolutely fed up with it after being here almost 12 months (about 7 days short of the year).'

The Oxfordshires were tasked to carry out a patrol into no-man's-land on the night of 15 July, and this time it was the turn of C Company's Second Lieutenant Godfrey Rawlinson to lead. The group was very small – just Rawlinson and four men – and they crept over the parapet just after midnight. Not long afterwards, Captain Edmonds, C Company's CO, was out in the fire trench inspecting his sentries when he heard whistling and cries for help. He hurriedly put together a rescue party from 10 Platoon and ventured out to where he had heard the sounds coming from. Groping around in the dark, Edmonds's party found Rawlinson, 'terribly wounded in the stomach',[80] with Private Cox dead nearby, 'practically on the German wire'. The Germans were watching for any potential rescue attempt, and suddenly Edmonds found himself under heavy attack. Showing superb resolve, the rescuers succeeded in getting Rawlinson back to safety, where he managed to tell what had happened. He had seen a light in the German trench and laid down to listen, but when he got up again the Germans spotted him and threw grenades, which was how he was wounded. As he went down, he saw two of his men captured and Cox dead, probably from the same grenade that had caught Rawlinson. The fate of the fourth man was unknown. Rawlinson played dead until things grew calm, when he began to whistle for help. He was evacuated to an advanced dressing station after making his report, but he died of his wounds the next day.

At long last, the Oxfordshires bade farewell to G Sector and Hébuterne, three days shy of a year after they had arrived in the area. They, and the rest of the 48th Division, were resubordinated to Sir Hubert Gough's Reserve Army, as part of X Corps. Handing over to the 10th Battalion, the Welsh Regiment, they marched away, 'hoping not to see those particular trenches again'. Jack saw how depleted the Welsh were, having just battled hard at Mametz Wood, with their platoons 'averaging about 12 strong', less than half their usual complement. Arriving at Couin at 1.00 a.m., the Oxfords were relieved to find lorries waiting to take them down to Bouzincourt, just to the north-west of Albert. As the trucks jarred and bumped their way along cratered roads crammed with marching troops, guns, horses, wagons and ambulances, Lidsey caught a glimpse of the 'Golden Virgin' leaning precariously from her perch atop Albert basilica. Legend had it that if she should topple, then whichever side knocked her down would lose the war. For now, though, she was still there – just. Looking at the other troops in town, Jack noticed jealously that 'everyone here seems to have two or three German helmets and dozens of other decent souvenirs, such as field glasses and watches'. Finding a stretcher for a bed in a hut, he settled in for the night. He was not to know it, but the Oxfordshires' time in the Battle of the Somme was about to come.

Tuesday July 18th
In morning had Communion Service in a Church Army hut. 7.30pm orders to move to battle at 8pm. Had hurried dinner. Marched to the scene of the action, going through Albert; passed right under the church tower and the Leaning Virgin. Scene of battle was left of

Ovillers. B and C Companys [sic] were doing the actual attack and A Company in support in the trench they went out from. Owing to the map being considerably incorrect, the attacking lines lost direction and ran into one of our own trenches which was at right-angles to the point of attack. They were fired on by machine-guns and obliged to retire. After daybreak the Huns subjected us to a very heavy fire of 5.9 shrapnel which was wonderfully well-timed, bursting about 6 feet over the trench. The trench was an absolute death trap, very shallow and affording us no cover. Twelve of my men were hit, of which three were killed. The Battalion casualties were about 110, A Company heading the list with over 40. We left the trench at 6am, going back down an old German trench we had captured; it was absolutely awful – we had to walk over dozens of bodies, half buried in the bottom of the trench, all in a high state of decay. The stench was awful and the sights terrifying; dozens of bodies all lying or thrown up onto the sides of the trench for about the three quarters of a mile that we passed through. Saw some of our mine craters – they were marvellous; it was impossible to see that there had been a trench there at all. Just huge craters in the ground, round which there were huge heaps of chalk and rubbish piled up thirty or forty feet high. Marched, or rather crawled, back to our huts at Bouzincourt.

The Oxfordshires had been ordered to attack, take, and hold a German trench, known as Sickle Trench (due to its shape, when viewed from above, resembling the handle and curved blade of the farming tool), which ran north-west at ninety degrees from the arrow-straight Albert to Bapaume Roman road between Ovillers-la-Boisselle and Pozières, before curving westwards towards Ovillers. It was a hastily organised operation: the time for the attack was specified as 1.30 a.m., leaving the battalion little time to prepare. There was no opportunity to reconnoitre the area, so they went in blind. What time they did have was spent drawing equipment, getting themselves to the start line and forming up for the attack – they made it to the start position with just fifteen minutes to spare before zero hour. The plan was for B Company to take the left side of the line with C Company to the right, and for A Company to

One of Jack Lidsey's wartime diaries. *(Lidsey Family Collection)*

Hardwick House, Banbury, Lidsey's childhood home. *(Courtesy Jane Pavia-Davis)*

Aerial view of Magdalen College School, Brackley; the school chapel is in the centre.

Above: Magdalen College School, Brackley. The main entrance, with the chapel in the background.
(Author's Collection)

Left: The Chapel of Saints James and John, Magdalen College School, Brackley. The School war memorial, paid for by the Stace family, is in front of the tower.
(Author's Collection)

Right: New recruits of the 1/4th (Oxfordshire) Battalion parade in an Oxford street, late August 1914. Jack Lidsey could well be in this picture.

Below: Soldiers of 1/4 (Oxfordshire) Battalion, The Oxfordshire & Buckinghamshire Light Infantry, in the town square of Hitchin, Hertfordshire, on 20 August 1914. The Battalion stopped in Hitchin en route to their training camp at Writtle. (*Courtesy Herts at War*)

The SS *Onward*, the ship that took the Oxfordshires to war on 29 March 1915.

Above: Soldiers of the Oxfordshire Battalion at rest in Ploegsteert Wood, spring 1915.

Left: Memorial plaque to the 1/4 (Oxfordshire) Battalion in Writtle, Essex, December 2018.
(*Courtesy Alicia Burton*)

Above: View towards the German lines from the eastern edge of Ploegsteert Wood, October 2018. The building in the right-centre distance was known as the 'White Estaminet'; the sandbag observation tower destroyed by a mountain gun on 12 May 1915 was to its right.
(*Courtesy Mark Banning*)

Left: Temporary Gentlemen: cadets of Number 5 OCB, Trinity College Cambridge, learning table manners at High Table.
(*Courtesy Barry Blades*)

Portrait of Jack Lidsey upon commissioning, May 1916. *(Lidsey Family Collection)*

Above left: Jack Lidsey in 1916, during the Battle of the Somme. Above right: Lidsey with an unknown officer (possibly Second Lieutenant H J Pullman) of the Buckinghamshire Battalion, 1916. The mud of the Somme is on their boots. *(Lidsey Family Collection)*

G Sector, just south-east of Hēbuterne looking east towards the German front line, September 2018. *(Author's Collection)*

Poziéres Cemetery, September 2018. Sickle Trench began here (on the Albert to Bapaume road) and followed the line of the central grass path. Many of the graves to the left of the path are those of men from the battalions of 145 Brigade killed whilst attacking the Trench in July 1916. *(Author's Collection)*

The location of Sickle Trench viewed from Ovillers-La-Boiselle looking towards Poziēres, September 2018. The rear of Poziéres Cemetery is on the horizon to the right; Sickle Trench ran from there into the centre of the picture, and then curved towards the camera. *(Author's Collection)*

Point 79, September 2018. The village of Thiepval is in the centre of the horizon, with the top of the Thiepval Memorial to the Missing visible above the trees to the left. *(Author's Collection)*

Left: The officers of A Company, 1/4 (Oxfordshire) Battalion, The Oxfordshire & Buckinghamshire Light Infantry, November 1916. Back row L-R: Jack Lidsey; Captain Jack Dimsdale Plowman (5th Middlesex); Unknown (possibly Second Lieutenant Archibald Allan); Captain Andrew Scott Wotherspoon (8th Scottish Rifles, The Cameronians). Front row L-R: Lieutenant H H Wrong; Captain F B Jones (Company CO); Lieutenant Tom Fortescue. *(Lidsey Family Collection)*

Below: An unexploded British Mills Bomb discovered by the author at Point 79, September 2018 – could it have been from Lidsey's bombing duel with the enemy on 23 August 1916? *(Author's Collection)*

Fokker Fodder – a Royal Aircraft Factory BE2e, serial number C7001, built by Barclay, Curle & Co Ltd in Glasgow. Note the wireless aerial cable spool alongside the pilot's cockpit. *(Imperial War Museum)*

An airworthy replica BE2e, based at Stow Maries Great War Aerodrome in Essex. *(by kind permission of David Davies)*

An air mechanic swings the propeller of a BE2 to start the engine; always a hazardous occupation that could lead to dismemberment or worse. *(16 Squadron)*

The Fokker *Eindecker*, scourge of the BE2 and game-changer in the skies over the Western Front in 1915.

Above left: Second Lieutenant Rodney Vernon Franklin, Jack Lidsey's first pilot. *(Australian War Memorial P12219.001)* Above right: Flight Sergeant Sidney Herbert Quicke in 1916; he wears the Observer's Badge, so this was taken before he qualified as a pilot. Right: Major Paul Copeland Maltby, Commanding Officer of 16 Squadron RFC, August 1916 – June 1917.

An aerial photograph of German trenches north of Fromelles taken by a 16 Squadron BE2 in 1916. Photographic reconnaissance was one of 16 Squadron's main tasks. *(Author's Collection)*

Manfred von Richthofen, the Red Baron.

Above: An Albatros D.V, similar to the D.III in which von Richthofen shot Lidsey and Quicke down. *(Author's Collection)* Right: Albatros D. IIIs of *Jasta 11* at La Brayelle, 1917. Von Richthofen's red-painted machine is second nearest the camera.

Hill 123, north of Neuville-St-Vaast, September 2018. Lidsey and Quicke's stricken BE2 crashed here on 21 March 1917. The trees in the distance on the right are on the top of Vimy Ridge. *(Author's Collection)*

Lidsey's original wooden grave cross on the wall of the chapel of Magdalen College School, Brackley. It has been renovated at some point in its history. Inset: Jack Lidsey's grave at Aubigny shortly after his burial. The photograph was taken at his family's behest and sent to them. *(Author's Collection)*

The grave of Second Lieutenant William John Lidsey at Aubigny, September 2018. *(Author's Collection)*

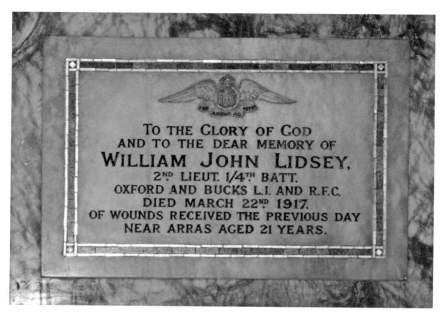

Above: The memorial plaque to Jack Lidsey inside St Mary's Church, Banbury, almost certainly placed there by his parents. Below: The grave of Flight Sergeant Sid Quicke at Bruay, September 2018.
(Author's Collection)

follow immediately behind in support to occupy the enemy trench once it had been taken. D Company was held in reserve.

The lack of reconnaissance was to prove disastrous. Having advanced just 100 yards from their start point, B Company on the left ran into another trench that was not marked on the map and that they had been unable to see in the dark. C Company saw what had happened and stopped. Both companies then jumped into a communication trench to re-form and get themselves reorganised so that they could continue the assault. All the while that this was going on, they were under constant enemy rifle fire from the left and enfilade machine-gun fire from the right. Unfortunately, A Company, who were following up as ordered but were completely unaware of the confusion going on in front of them, then ran into the other two companies. German artillery now opened fire, showering the shambolic mass of Oxfordshires with shrapnel rounds and causing many casualties since the trench they were sheltering in was narrow and shallow, offering little in the way of protection. It was clear by now that the attack had failed. A second assault was ordered but, due to the increasing amount of casualties, the confusion and the exposed position, it was called off at 4.15 a.m. and the Oxfordshires were ordered to withdraw. There was no order to their retreat, with the men stumbling rearwards dazed and shocked in disorganised, leaderless groups. The battalion War Diary lists a total of two officers wounded; twelve other ranks killed; another four missing, believed wounded; eighty-two wounded; and one missing.[81] Several of those wounded later died, bringing the total dead in the assault on Sickle Trench to twenty. The next morning, Jack 'did the painful and unpleasant duty of writing to the next-of-kin of my casualties'.

Sickle Trench had to be taken, given its commanding position overlooking the main road right in the centre of the British line of advance and protecting the approach to Pozières, the highest point on the battlefield. A second attack was ordered for the night of 20–21 July, this time by the Buckinghamshires alongside the Gloucestershires, with the Oxfordshires in reserve. Lidsey assembled his weary men and they marched off at 11.45 p.m. to their holding position just outside Albert, waiting to move forward if called upon. The Germans were alert to the fact that they would probably be attacked again – they too knew the importance of Sickle Trench – and were waiting for the British. At 2.45 a.m. the Bucks and Glosters advanced into a hail of enemy machine-gun fire: 'They ran up against awful odds; nearly all who went over the parapet were wiped out by MG fire which came from the front and flank. We were in support; fortunately, were not called upon. It was afterwards that we found that the line we attempted to attack was not an insignificant trench, but the old main Prussian defence. Poor old Trimmer,[82] my pal in the Bucks, was killed.'

A few isolated men did apparently reach the enemy line, but hardly any returned. Again, the attack had failed, and the Bucks and Glosters withdrew leaving behind 12 killed, 100 wounded and over 40 missing.

Pozières was by now the main effort for the British. The village had to be captured as quickly as possible if the entire Somme battle was to keep moving. A major assault was ordered for the night of 22–23 July with the 1st Australian Division attacking from the south of the village while the 48th Division would support them from the west. The Oxfordshires were to attack beyond Sickle Trench, almost up to the main German trench line in front of Pozières itself. By way of encouragement, the 48th Division's CO, Major General Robert Fanshawe, sent his soldiers a rallying message:

The Major-General recognises how very gallant and determined the attacks were which the Battalions made in the last few days, and how very nearly they succeeded completely. Those who took part in them may well be proud of their effort to break the German line here. Those in the Brigades who were not engaged may be equally proud of their comrades and the Brigade and Battalion Commanders and staff of having trained and directed such efforts. Great successes have indeed already been gained by us. We must make one more effort and take advantage of all we have learned about the position and show the Germans that in spite of all the difficulties and dangers, we are going to beat them. A victory gained after great efforts will be more really decisive as showing we are better fighting men than if we had gained it at our first attempt. The decisive fights which lead to final victory are not those easily gained, but those which, like the first battle of Ypres, are gained by the determination to win no matter the odds in number and difficulties against us. Here we are up against a strong position, the best German troops, machine guns and artillery fire; let our determination to win carry us through.[83]

It is not hard to imagine the likely reaction of the Oxfordshires when the message was read out to the troops.

A Company was to take the left flank of the Oxfordshires' advance. Jack Lidsey once more assembled 3 Platoon and issued his orders for their part of the attack, and they moved off at 8.00 p.m. on the Saturday night towards their start line. Zero hour was just after midnight on the morning of Sunday 23 July:

> Started advancing at 12.30am. Crossed one Hun trench with very little resistance, then found ourselves enfiladed by two machine-guns, one on each flank. We lay there for half an hour as we did not know where we were; sent two runners back to find the Company CO – in about half an hour's time we received orders to go back the way we came. We then attacked and took a Hun trench a little further to the north; we were immediately counter-attacked three times. The men fought and used bombs admirably. By this time, we were very much cut-up; I had only one sergeant and three men left of my Platoon. We ran short of bombs – the situation was fast getting serious when we were reinforced by the Berkshires who brought plenty of bombs. They bombed the Huns out further north while we consolidated our position. We were shelled very heavily; we escaped very lightly. During the day about 100 Huns were cornered in a trench; they broke cover and ran for it up between two lines of trenches. We got Lewis Guns on to them; those that were not killed (about 30) surrendered to the Bucks and were immediately marched off. Hung on to the trench all day.

Lidsey's near-extinct platoon did indeed 'hang on' to their part of the captured trench – but only just. At one point during the desperate strug-gle, one of his men, Lance Corporal T. Ward, single-handedly held off a German bombing party for ten minutes while Jack frantically searched

for more bombs and organised a fresh attack against the enemy. Ward
rightly won the Military Medal for his bravery, but it seems odd that Jack
was not awarded some sort of recognition for his leadership that day.
The battalion War Diary records that the attack by the Oxfordshires' left,
led by Lidsey's 3 Platoon, was 'a hard struggle'. Of the enemy counter-
attacks, the War Diary says: 'Half an hour before dawn, the enemy got
onto their parapet, right and left of Point 11, and advanced several times
in close formation, but were driven back by our Lewis Gun and rifle
fire. Another counter-attack took place about the same time from Point
43; this was only tried once and was easily driven back.'[84]

Exhausted and severely depleted, the Oxfordshires were relieved
by the Warwickshires at 1.00 a.m. on 24 July, having been in action
continuously for over 24 hours:

> More than glad to get away; marched back to our camp north of
> Albert – arrived there dead tired and <u>slept</u>. This trench had been
> attacked by the British no less than six times previously; it takes
> the Oxfords to do it. A Company did all the work, consequently had
> the most casualties. Two machine guns, three hundred and fifty
> prisoners and a quantity of gas apparatus were taken by our
> Brigade. Of course, the Oxfords are again mentioned in despatches.
> Generals very pleased. 3.15pm marched back to our hutments at
> Bouzincourt; were welcomed by the Divisional band. Had a good
> wash, a good feed and then <u>slept some sleep</u>.

At last, the aptly named Sickle Trench and its supporting lines were in
British hands, but at a substantial cost. The Oxfordshire Battalion lost 5
officers and 74 other ranks killed, with a further 150 wounded, that night
and the following day. They had suffered so heavily that a reorganisation
needed to be carried out, moving men from one company to another to
make up some of the numbers; C Company was 'practically the only
Company with any NCOs left'.[85] Once the figures across the 48th Division
as a whole had been consolidated, from 16 to 28 July they had taken
over 2,800 casualties. The Australians fought hard for Pozières over the
next few days, eventually succeeding in driving the Germans out of what
was left of the village, again at a horrendous cost and winning four

Victoria Crosses in the process.

After their horrific time in front of Pozières, the Oxfordshires were moved away from the front to rest and recuperate. They left Bouzincourt on 26 July, marching seven miles north-west to Arquèves, well away from the fighting. Camping out in an orchard under warm summer skies and having complete rest, the next couple of days were 'very welcome'.

They moved again on the 28th, this time to Beauval. Jack stopped along the way to collect the first batch of replacement troops, although ten men did not seem anywhere near adequate to compensate for the losses of the last week. The fresh soldiers were conscripts and, at first, were eyed with scorn by the original Oxfords who had been through so much together and lost so many comrades. The new billets at Beauval proved to be worth the march, though, and Lidsey found a real bed – 'the first since being out here this time' – and electricity waiting for him, and consequently, he had 'a first-rate sleep'. The good night's rest was to prove much-needed, as the Oxfordshires moved yet again the next morning, making a fifteen-mile hike in sweltering heat to Agenville, even further away from the Somme battlefront. Arriving in the early afternoon, dripping with sweat, Jack nevertheless declared himself as feeling 'wonderfully fit' although that was to change when he found his billet: 'extremely dirty; there is a bed, but it looks as though it is full of lice; that remains to be proved. Managed to borrow a bivvy sheet, so hurriedly quitted our lousy billet. Found two lice on me before I had been there 10 minutes – they were committed to the thumb nail. Fortunately did not bring any more away with me. Rigged up a very good bivvy in a first-rate orchard just by our Mess billet. Very comfortable – much better than being indoors in this weather.'

The warm weather held, and they stayed at Agenville for the next ten days. The long, hot days were spent either resting or training, with a combination of drill, rifle practice and physical exercise. More replacement troops arrived; slowly, the battalion was getting itself back on to its feet. Jack had the opportunity for some time off, travelling in the mess cart to Abbeville near the coast where he bought some watercolours of local scenes to send home, and some 'jolly fine cream cheeses; just ripe, nice and high, and also crawly'. The gesture wasn't appreciated by his fellow billet occupants, though, who found the cheeses far too ripe and smelly for comfort, so 'I had to eat them all alone'.

The rest period could not last. As the fighting troops at the front were rotated, it was soon the Oxfordshires' turn once more and they began moving forward on Wednesday 9 August 1916. In 'terrific heat' and a 'continual cloud of dust', they marched to Beauval again, with several men succumbing to heat exhaustion along the way: 'nearly done up. Rather a lot of men fell out, including five from my platoon – the worst I have ever had. Of course, four of them were reinforcements; have not had time to "break them in" yet.'

The next day, they moved again, this time to Varennes. Leaving at 5.00 a.m., it rained the whole way, and they found themselves in 'very bad billets. Slept on a brick floor in farmhouse kitchen.' Then at 4.00 a.m. the following morning it was on to Bouzincourt, within range of the German artillery once more. As soon as the Oxfordshires arrived, they were welcomed back by a hail of 5.9 shells.

Jack's luck was in, however. Almost as soon as they had arrived he was given orders to attend a Lewis Gun course at a training school on the coast, at Paris-Plage, Le Touquet. He was 'very bucked at being able to escape a few days at Pozières, which is by no means healthy'. He set off straight away, arriving the next evening, on 12 August. The course lasted six days, and Lidsey found it 'very interesting', especially the live firing exercises with 'the very fine sight of 100 Lewis Guns firing into the sandbank all at once. There was a terrific roar and then a huge cloud of sand about 600 yards long flew into the air.' There was time to swim in the sea, and to sample the seafront restaurants in the fashionable Paris-Plage area. He got back to Bouzincourt on the 20th, where he learned that 'the Battalion had had two very rough turns in the trenches, including an attack and a counter-attack whilst I had been away, so I <u>had</u> missed something. Poor Wayman is missing, Hunter killed and several others wounded.'

Lidsey had certainly 'missed something'. The Oxfords had moved into the front line north-west of Pozières on 13 August, taking over a trench known as Skyline Trench (overlooking the village of Thiepval, an objective on 1 July that was still to be taken) from the Norfolks and the Essexes, who had captured it the previous night and which was still hotly contested – German troops could be heard talking a matter of a few yards away in the communications trenches that ran off Skyline Trench. The last 300 yards of the route into the trench proved hazardous since it was covered by a German sniper who had already killed four that morning. The incoming Oxfords had to press themselves flat to the earth and crawl all the way, working around the bodies of the sniper's victims – the journey took over an hour. Once in the supposed safety of Skyline, they found the wounded from the previous night's attack who had dragged themselves into the shelter of the old German dugouts, with their moans and cries for water only adding to the sense of unease. There was no fire-step facing the enemy since this was a German trench, meaning the fire-step was on the wrong side (facing back towards the British rear), so to watch the enemy, they had to attach mirrors to their bayonets and raise them above the parapet, fixed to their rifles. As they settled them-selves in, one man of the Oxfordshires found the tension too much to bear and started out over the parapet in tears, saying he wanted to go home. The enemy sniper swiftly claimed another victim.

Almost as soon as the relief was complete, the enemy shelled the trench, with it 'being obliterated by the evening'.[86] Casualties were heavy, but the Germans were not finished yet. At around 9.00 p.m., they counter-attacked Skyline in strength in an attempt to re-take it. Their assault was detected while it was still forming up and D Company, who were facing the build-up, sent five messages back to Battalion HQ requesting support, but none of the runners got through. The Oxfordshires' line was pierced in the centre, but a gallant action by Second Lieutenant Charles Sherrington (with whom Jack had travelled when he rejoined the Oxfordshires after commissioning back in May) of D Company held the enemy at bay. Sherrington's platoon was practically surrounded and was in danger of being cut off and captured, so he decided to withdraw further back down the trench and regroup. On the way, he stumbled upon Lance Corporal Hermon, a Lewis Gunner who was attempting to hold the left flank alone as the rest of his section had already retreated. Sherrington stayed with Hermon to act as his ammunition man, until Hermon was shot through the eye. Instead of retiring further, Sherrington manned the Lewis Gun on his own, succeeding in securing the battalion's left flank and allowing what was left of his platoon to with-draw. For his actions, Sherrington was awarded the Military Cross.[87] The citation for his medal stated that 'his masterly withdrawal in the face of onerous odds kept the line intact and enabled a counter-attack afterwards to regain more easily the position evacuated'.[88] Sherrington himself thought that he was to be court-martialled for 'retreating against orders', or running away from the enemy, which he genuinely felt to be the case.[89] Lance Corporal Hermon, a milkman from Henley described by Sherrington as 'inordinately brave', won the Military Medal but did not live to receive it. He died of his wounds in hospital in Rouen ten days later.

Meanwhile, the survivors of two platoons from C Company on the right flank, under Sergeant Crowe, were cut off from the rest of the battalion. Gathering those still able to fight around him, Crowe led repeated bombing attacks down the trench against the Germans who had suc-ceeded in getting into his section of the line. With their ammunition and bombs running low, Crowe's dwindling party managed to hold out for twenty-four hours until relieved the following night, thereby preventing the enemy from breaking through and consolidating their gains. Sergeant Crowe won the Distinguished Conduct Medal that day, second only to the Victoria Cross.

The two officers that Jack mentioned, Wayman and Hunter, were Captain William Wayman of A Company and Lieutenant Leslie Hunter of C Company; the bodies of neither man were ever found. Thirty-year-old Leslie Hunter was an Old Wykehamist and had been a brilliant scholar. A fellow and lecturer of New College, Oxford, he had only arrived with the Oxfordshires on 7 August and was dead just a week later. The day that he died had been Hunter's first ever in the trenches; despite his complete inexperience, his company commander had had no choice but to put him in charge of a bombing party because there were no other unwounded officers left to lead it. When a more seasoned officer did eventually arrive to take over from him, Hunter refused to be relieved and was killed by a German grenade soon after.

Battered and exhausted, the Oxfords were replaced on the afternoon on 14 August, moving back towards Albert for a very brief rest. Their brave defence of Skyline Trench had cost them 53 dead, with a further 100 miss-ing or wounded. They were called forward again almost immediately, moving back into Skyline and its supporting position, Ration Trench,

on the 16th. There they stayed for two days, during which they were continually shelled, taking more casualties. A second German counter-attack
was foiled when the Oxfordshires spotted it while it was assembling
and called for an artillery barrage on the enemy position. A prisoner captured shortly afterwards ('an educated man, 24 years of age, who was a
student of Bonn University at the outbreak of the war'[90]) confirmed it
was the British shelling that had broken up the intended German assault.

   As Jack absorbed the news of what his men had been through in his
absence, the Oxfordshires rested themselves, knowing that they would
soon be called upon again. And so it was to be – they moved back into
the fire trenches on the morning of 23 August, this time a little to the
left of Skyline Trench, again overlooking Thiepval, close to a German
strongpoint at a trench junction known as Point 79:

> Very hot bit of trench too, with both our flanks 'in the air'[91]; the left
> flank is a 'bomb stop' where we are continually bombing and being
> bombed. First we push them back a little and then they push us
> back; it is some 'hot shop'. Had a very lively night; were bombing
> on the left all night and digging a trench on our right to try to get
> a connection with the Company on our right; of course had
> numerous casualties at the bombing. The communications trench
> was also very unhealthy as the Huns shelled it all night with 5.9s.
> My servant and I had a near go[92] several times, one of which he was
> knocked unconscious.

Lidsey was at the centre of the fiercest fighting throughout that attack.
The battalion War Diary records that 'bombing at this Point [was] continuous throughout the next 48 hours', and that there was 'constant touch
at Point 79 with enemy; actual trench junction too strongly held by the
enemy [and] could not be forced by direct bombing attacks alone'.[93]
The bombing duel resulted in A Company gaining about thirty yards of
trench from the Germans, bringing them to within twenty yards of Point
79, before they handed over to D Company at noon the next day. Jack
was 'very pleased to get away, if only for a short distance. The continual
bombing tried us very much, and we came out very tired and not a little
shaken.' Moving out of the front line, he found himself somewhere to

rest close by in a dugout down a communications trench, still with the
sounds of battle raging all around him. He was shaken awake at 11.00 p.m.
by a runner delivering a message for him to report to Captain Jones, the
A Company CO, who ordered Lidsey to take his two bombing sections
up to the bomb stop, advance and capture Point 79:

> It was an impossible task; the men were tired out and very few
> of them were bombers at all. We carried our bombs up there and
> were just about to start to commit suicide when an order came by
> messenger that I was not to attack. They at last see the folly of trying
> to take it in this manner. This, by the way, would have been the third
> time that I have attacked 79, the two previous attempts of course
> being failures. Returned to our dug-outs – which by the way were
> very deep German ones that we had captured – more tired than
> ever. We were too crowded to get much rest, to say nothing of the
> hordes of fleas.

Twice that day, the 24th, the Oxfords readied themselves to attack Point
79 and twice they were ordered to stand down. The first time, at 4.00 p.m.,
they were pulled back to allow for a bombardment against the position
by British heavy artillery. The second time, described above by Lidsey,
was because of the sheer strength of the enemy defences; as well as
reinforcing the front-line trench, the Germans had established machine-
gun positions in the craters made by the afternoon's shelling.

   The pressure and intensity of battle in the Ovillers–Thiepval area were
relentless. Even when at rest out of the fire trenches, the Oxfordshires
were never more than a few hundred yards from the front line, and
constantly under German artillery fire. In 'disgracefully inadequate'
dugouts behind Ovillers on 26 August, crowded in 'like herrings', Lidsey
and his men slept 'because we were too tired to keep awake' despite the
heavy shelling. Patrols sent out to assess the German defences around
Point 79 reported the 'enemy digging energetically and [the front] line
strongly held'.[94] Again, Jack and the rest of A Company were sent forward, this time to support the Berkshires in yet another attempt at taking
Point 79. They advanced at 7.00p.m. on the 27th, and this time:

The attack was a complete success, the whole objective being gained, which of course included 'the worry of my life for the last three days' – Point 79. About sixty prisoners, including four officers, were captured; also a machine-gun, to say nothing of equipment, bombs, rifle and trench stores. The Fifth Prussian Guard[95] were against us; they had been practically starved for five days as our artillery was so hot on their communication trenches that they could not get up supplies. A Company were carrying bombs and sand-bags up to the captured trench all night.

One of the German prisoners had been at Verdun and declared to his captors that it was 'a flea bite compared to this place'. At long last, on the 28th and in pouring rain that was to persist for the rest of the month, the Oxfords, and indeed the entire South Midland Division, were pulled out of the line for a proper rest, leaving behind a further thirteen men dead from the final attack on Point 79. As they made their weary way back to the rear in the deluge, a passing Australian soldier shouted to Jack, 'What Division are you?', '48th,' Lidsey replied. The 'digger', no doubt well aware that it was the 48th who had fought alongside the Australians at Pozières, responded with irony, 'Is that the only Division in the bloody British Army?'

Nine miles later, they arrived at Bus-lès-Artois to find that their billets were 'beastly, rotten huts which are by no means waterproof and which do not contain a stick of furniture [the huts had been stripped bare by their previous occupants], not even a box to put our food on. Feeling very fed up. Very heavy thunderstorm; practically flooded out, all our belongings wet through.' The next day, though, buoyed by the news that Romania had declared war on Germany, Jack observed somewhat optimistically that 'we have the Hun by the scrotum; it is now only a matter of time'.

During the murderous assaults on, and subsequent courageous defences of, Sickle and Skyline Trenches and Point 79 during July and August 1916, the 1/4 (Oxfordshire) Battalion won three Military Crosses (including Sherrington's and one by the battalion's padre, the Reverend K.C. Jackson, for evacuating wounded men while under fire), three Distinguished Conduct Medals and eight Military Medals. The actions had cost them 173 men killed – they had started July with a fighting strength of 36 officers and 1,072 other ranks, but at the end of August, even with replacements, they were down to 22 officers and 800 men.

Chapter Eight

The Somme, 1 September – 22 November 1916

Finally, the weather improved and A Company set about trying to dry their saturated uniforms and to recuperate after their time at the front. The whole battalion was inspected by the divisional commander, Major General Robert Fanshawe, on 2 September. Fanshawe gave a speech thanking the Oxfordshires for what they had done during July and August but reminded them that there was still much to do. Despite being in the rear, the sound of war was still there with them – at church the next day, Sunday, the noise of the guns of the artillery firing was so great that 'we could barely hear ourselves speaking during the Communion service'.

All too soon, the Oxfordshires' time in the rear was over. Orders arrived on Tuesday 5 September sending them into the line again, this time thankfully to a 'peaceful' stretch just to the east of Auchonvillers (known as 'Ocean Villas' to the Tommies), looking down on the village of Beaumont-Hamel. Leaving Bus at 8.30 a.m., the battalion marched to Mailly-Maillet where they left their packs before continuing to the trenches. A Company went straight into the fire trenches, relieving the men of the 7th Worcesters around noon. Jack was pleasantly surprised to find that their new home, on the right of the line, was 'the best trenches that I have ever been in, provided it does not rain much as the soil is very soft and sandy'. He also found 'plenty of first-class dug-outs, after the style of the Germans but much better, made by the British REs[96] – not by the 48th Div RE though as they are too damned lazy to make the infantry safe and comfortable. Trenches full of gas cylinders; the trenches stink of it.'

Despite the relative peace – the Worcesters had only suffered one lightly wounded casualty during their ten-day stint – Lidsey found himself feeling uneasy. He knew that their trench had been undermined by the Germans and was 'consequently liable to go up into thin air at any minute'. Hoping that his platoon would not be the unfortunate occupants if and when the Germans decided to blow the trench up from underground, Jack found a crumb of consolation in the fact that the enemy was in the same predicament, with British tunnellers working deep beneath their positions.

The benign conditions continued the next day, and Lidsey was further buoyed up by the arrival of 'tons of fruit and wine' from Amiens, and a parcel from home containing Banbury cakes[97] and chocolate (throughout the war, Magdalen College School, Brackley, pupils subscribed to tuck-boxes 'containing fruit, vegetables and home-made cakes' that were sent to the school's old boys who were serving with the Oxfordshire Battalion[98]). Even a strafe in the evening by German trench mortars did nothing more than 'put the wind up' 3 Platoon, with most of the rounds landing harmlessly in no-man's-land. Settling back to enjoy the comforts from home, the Oxfordshires could hear a battle off to their right, towards Pozières, but thankfully it was far enough away not to trouble them.

At 9.00 a.m. on Friday 8 September, after just three days, Lidsey's latest turn in the line ended when he and his men were relieved by the 1/4 Royal Berkshires. Pleased not to have taken any casualties, and no doubt thankful that the Germans had not blown their subterranean mine while they were in residence, the Oxfordshires marched back to Bus in excellent weather, where Jack found his billet to be 'fair to middling'. A couple of days later, the Oxfords returned to their old billets in Beauval, revelling in the fact that their heavy packs had been sent on by motor transport and that a recent shower had dampened down the dust and cooled the air. Life was almost tolerable again.

There is nothing in Jack Lidsey's wartime diaries that suggests any interest in a flying career whatsoever. There are a few references to watching aerial combat from the trenches, such as his entry for Monday 26 April 1915 when at Ploegsteert:

During afternoon a British aeroplane flew very low just over and along the line of German trenches under a terrific hail of shells and bullets, when just opposite us and beyond the enemy's trenches the machine came down to within about 5 yards of the ground. The Bosches were all firing at it full steam; must have been positively riddled with bullets. Suddenly after we had given up all hope, he rose again and flew right away; roars of cheering from our trenches – we all got in a bunch and shouted 'how's that, Fritz?' (German trenches 150 yards away).

On Wednesday 1 September 1915, he wrote:

At about 10am watched a very exciting duel between two airmen, which had an unfortunate ending. The British machine had outmanoeuvred the German; it was flying about directly over him when suddenly the German very cleverly tilted his machine right on one side, at the same time getting his machine gun on our machine; one bullet evidently pierced the petrol tank of our aeroplane, as almost immediately she began to descend and did a spiral descent right to earth. The German followed his descent all the way down so as to be sure he wasn't shamming. It is the first British machine I have seen brought down.

And this, on Thursday 16 July 1916:

Watched the best air fight I have ever seen, it was some way towards the Hun lines. Saw two of our large planes flying over towards the Hun lines. Soon after I heard a large quantity of machine gun fire in the air. Looked up and saw the most exciting scrap I have ever seen, unfortunately they were too far away to see well. There were five Fokkers against our two machines. All seven machines dived and wheeled and dived and wheeled and fired machine guns for nearly a quarter of an hour.

But such entries are rare, and in any case, the first two were made early on in his war when seeing aeroplanes was a novelty. Any other comments about aircraft are made in passing – straightforward, nondescript observations about the comings and goings of machines of both sides, going about their business as if they were wagons or lorries. At no point does Jack express any desire to fly, or to join the Royal Flying Corps; indeed, from the start of the Battle of the Somme, his diary is, as we have seen, full of detail about the ground fighting he was involved with. So, it is somewhat of a surprise to come across his diary entry for Tuesday 12 September 1916. A simple, matter-of-fact, single sentence that day, that reads: 'I presented my application for a transfer to the RFC.'

What drove this request? Lidsey himself gives no clues. If he was eager to escape the trenches, then nothing in what he had written up to that point tells us so. It would have been no revelation had he confided to his diary that he wanted to find a way out as he had been in action for some considerable time by that stage. There was a feeling among the infantry that the Royal Flying Corps had it easy, as there were no muddy trenches or waterlogged dugouts, no constant shelling, and no inter-minable marches to and from the front line. Instead, there were proper beds in decent billets, and a mess with hot food every day. But the tone and candour of Jack's diary entries had not changed with time; just the day before his application went in, he tells us that he had spent a good night in a comfortable billet; 'very nice too, bed and electric light; beautifully clean'.

He must also have surely known that his chances of survival as an airman were no better, if not worse, than those as an infantry officer at that point in the war, even if the living conditions were better. On aver-age, the life expectancy of RFC aircrew was around eighteen hours' flying time; given that a sortie lasted about two hours, a flyer would be dead after just nine trips. It was not solely the enemy that was to blame for this condensed lifespan, but also the unreliability of early aeroplanes, a lack of training and basic to nonexistent safety systems. Lidsey's motives are a mystery. Perhaps the one thing that gives a sign of his state of mind is a group photograph taken in November 1916 of the A Company officers. While none of the seven men in the picture look particularly happy – only the company CO, Captain Jones, manages a half-smile – Lidsey, standing top left, looks gaunt and drawn, especially when compared to the portrait of him done shortly after commissioning just a few months previously. Gone are the youthful looks; he has aged, lost weight and his uniform is battered and worn. He wears the expression of what soldiers call the 'thousand-yard stare' – the vacant and haunted eyes of someone who has been exposed to the horrors of war for too long.

Even after his RFC application on 12 September, his writing continues in the same vein, with barely a mention of anything flying-related. He does pay a couple of visits to a nearby airfield, but the only time he goes into any detail (although hardly effusive) is on 19 September when he 'chatted with the pilots and watched the planes rising and alighting; very interesting indeed. Saw one of the new Spad planes; they are French, very fast, climb 6,000ft in 5 minutes.'

Lidsey had a medical for the RFC on 16 September and was found to be fit for flying duties; all he had to do now was wait for his interview. In the meantime, Jack spent his time at the brigade Bombing School, learning about German bombs and the operation of the Stokes mortar, a British weapon for lobbing mortar rounds into enemy trenches. In preparation for the RFC, he also began to learn Morse code, noting with some satisfaction that he could manage six words a minute.

The battalion moved accommodation on 18 September, marching six miles westwards in a downpour to Fienvillers. Jack and his fellow officers arrived soaked through at their billet, a house in the village, only to discover that the elderly landlady refused to let them in:

The old girl would not have us in at any price; we went to fetch the priest for assistance. He told her that he would fetch the gendarmes if she would not have us; after that she consented. It appears that she is 86 and the sole occupant of the house, however we made a fuss of her and she is a jolly good old sport, does everything she can to make us comfortable, finds us firewood and blankets, and chats to us all day long. She evidently had some rotters here before who had treated her badly. Sleeping on a stretcher in the attic; very comfortable too.

The bombing course continued, even in the pouring rain. Time was spent throwing live Mills bombs and digging practice bombing trenches, a pursuit that Jack considered a 'useless occupation'. On 22 September, a round of inoculations against typhoid was dished out by the medical orderlies, causing Lidsey's arm to become stiff and sore, feeling like 'it was being beaten with a hammer all the time'. The adverse reaction also gave him a fever, confining him to his bed until it passed the next day. When he was up and about, Jack was detailed to attend a lecture on sanitation, 'including flies, germs and diseases. It was very interesting indeed, but extremely revolting.'

Over the few next days, news and gossip began to filter in from both the Somme battlefront and home. The newspapers of 25 September reported the bringing down of two Zeppelins over Essex. Zeppelin L32 was shot down near Billericay, with L33 crashing near Little Wigborough after being hit by anti-aircraft fire. Added to this 'great news' came reports of thirty German aircraft downed over France. Lidsey gives a hint of what regimental mess life was like for a Temporary Gentleman in his diary entry that day, when he expresses his delight that 'Tom Fortescue [who led the abortive trench raid the night before the Somme offensive began] returned from Rouen. Very glad to have him back after having had to listen to classical talk at Mess for about two months. It will be considerably more cheerful now.'[99] Presumably discussing the classics with former public schoolboys was a level above what the ex-grammar school boy was comfortable with.

On the ground, the third phase of the Battle of the Somme continued and the rumours were rife, and although Jack declared that he had got past taking any notice of them by now, he was thrilled to hear that Morval, Flers and Gueudecourt had fallen. The reports this time were true – the British Fourth Army, with the French Sixth Army to their right, had indeed advanced, inflicting severe casualties on the Germans and capturing several key villages. The penetration was the greatest achieved by the Fourth Army since 14 July, but a combination of bad weather, slow progress by the French and a lack of reserves eventually meant that the gains were not as great as they might have been. Still, the Germans had been pushed back, closer to Bapaume.

Rumours also reached Lidsey that Thiepval had been taken, but this was not yet the case. Although the Battle of Thiepval Ridge had started on 26 September with initial gains, the final objectives were not taken until early October during the Battle of the Ancre Heights.

On 27 September, Lidsey had a rare day off and decided to take a trip into Amiens, along with Second Lieutenant Guy Ramsay of the Cameronians (Scottish Rifles) who was attached to the Oxfordshires. Their train from Candas was delayed for an hour, so they headed for an estaminet and ordered a bottle of vin blanc and made good use of the piano while they drank. Finally arriving in Amiens at midday, the pair had a good lunch before taking a much-needed bath and shampoo, and then a spot of sightseeing around Amiens cathedral. Afterwards, they decided to do some shopping. While Jack was browsing a shop window, he suddenly became aware of a commotion behind him. Turning sharply, he was horrified to see Ramsay convulsing in an apparent epileptic fit. Catching his companion as he fell, Jack shouted to one of the gawping crowd of off-duty Tommies to fetch a doctor. As luck would have it, two of the onlookers were French Army doctors and they ran to help. While the medics treated the unfortunate Ramsay, Lidsey hailed a passing ambulance, which sped the patient to the nearby 1st New Zealand Stationary Hospital where he was at once hospitalised:

It frightened me just a bit at the time; I had never seen a fit of that sort before. He fell without a word, shook with convulsions all over, foamed at the mouth, and went a ghastly colour. It was a very unpleasant day's outing. When I left him to catch my train, he seemed to have completely lost his memory, asked whether he was in England or France, what regiment he was in, and who I was and lots more such questions.

Lidsey was late back to his billet that night as he had stayed on to comfort his friend in the hospital. He reached Candas at midnight, and then walked to Fienvillers only to be woken a few hours later for a day's field training, which lasted until 1.00 a.m. the following morning.

An orderly shook Jack awake just four hours later with orders that the battalion was to move at 9.00 a.m. Exhausted from the previous day's manoeuvres, his mood was further darkened by the discovery that it was pouring with rain. Trudging through the abysmal weather, they marched until 1.00 p.m. when they stopped at the roadside for lunch. Moving off again an hour later, they arrived, soaked through, at Warluzel, south-west of Arras, having covered some twelve miles to get there. Still, the billet was adequate, if a little dirty. The rumour was that they would soon go back into the line at Hébuterne, their old stamping ground, and Lidsey remarked sardonically that it would be 'quite like home again'. Now, though, they were no longer part of the Reserve Army, but found themselves in VII Corps of the British Third Army under General Sir Edmund Allenby.

October 1916 arrived with the news that the Oxfordshires were to move yet again, this time to Warlincourt, eight miles to the south. Another march, and when they got there they found that their billets were still occupied. Finding some old huts that were far from weather-proof, Lidsey dumped his kit and, fatigued from the previous few days, turned in early, observing that the accommodation was so poor that he 'shall have a thin time of it, if it rains much'. Which of course it then did, continuously for the next three days and nights. In all, the battalion spent eighteen days at Warlincourt, with not much to do other than practise for an attack on Gommecourt Wood, which was then cancelled. Time not in training was spent playing plenty of football, and watching Charlie Chaplin films in a nearby French barn, dubbed the 'Grand Palace Cinema'.

On the morning of 12 October, Jack rode on a pack pony to Doullens to be interviewed by a Royal Flying Corps major. He found a 'whole crowd' waiting, so went away and came back after 'a very poor' lunch, eventually to be seen at 2.30 p.m. The interview was thorough and covered every aspect of his life up to that point, with each answer being carefully noted down. Lidsey did well enough to pass and was told that he should go on three weeks' probation with the RFC and was put on a waiting list to be an observer.

Back at Warlincourt the next day, Jack took part in bayonet practice with his platoon, which proved a hazardous undertaking: 'very narrowly escaped being struck whilst sparring with one of my men; I will leave him alone in the future. He is good enough for any Bosche; he is the Platoon's "father" – 41 years old.'

Another series of marches and moves marked the second half of the month, first from Warlincourt back to Warluzel on the 19th, then ten miles to Beauval on the 22nd, and six miles to Talmas the following day before finally moving again on the 24th by a roundabout route to

Lahoussoye, midway between Albert and Amiens. The last leg was made in the pouring rain, and once again they arrived at their destination wet through, having marched fourteen miles along bad roads, which, had they gone by a more direct route, could have been reached in half the distance. The billets were comfortable but crowded, with Jack sharing a small room with six other officers, although he was 'very comfortable and contented'. All was not well in his men's billet, however, and he was called to deal with an incident between them and the owners:

> They [his soldiers] lit a brazier much to the annoyance of the old man and woman, who at once took steps to extinguish it. The old girl snatched up a bucket and filled it with filthy water from a cesspool, rushed across the barn, steering for the brazier. However, in her rage, she fails to see a sack of coal in which she caught her foot, fell flat on the floor and swilled herself with the stinking water; serve her right too, miserable old devil. The first attack was followed up immediately by a second – the old man rushed up with his bucket; he was so furious that he missed his aim and threw the water on a heap of thrashed corn. Of course, this made him madder than ever; he continued his mad rush and gave the brazier a boot with his foot, eventually kicking it out of the barn, and it was with great difficulty that we prevented a fire. I then arrived on the scene with the interpreter, who ticked the old boy off pretty forcibly. It did not take long to get the fire burning again. It was well worth the fun.

On 28 October, a Saturday, Lidsey, in company with his friend Tom Fortescue and a captain named Andrew Wotherspoon, another Cameronian officer attached to the Oxfords, rode on a GS wagon into Amiens. It was Jack's first day off in a month. Arriving 'nearly shaken to pieces', the trio spent the day shopping and dining. They 'lunched very sumptuously at the Salon Gourbet, to the tune of 60 francs', before heading back to the battalion at 9.00 p.m. As they resigned themselves to a long walk in the dark, they 'had the luck to be overtaken by a lorry which we stopped and managed to squeeze into. It was packed full of Australians, all of whom were very drunk. It was a fearful crush, but a thousand times better than "paddling the 'oof" for about ten miles.

Arrived back at Lahoussoye at 10pm.'

The Oxfordshires had only just bedded themselves in at Lahoussoye when inevitably word came to move again. Millencourt was seven miles away, and about two miles from Albert. This time the march was completed in decent weather, albeit along main roads thick with military traffic. The new billet was dirty and rat-infested, and run by a curious old woman who kept a menagerie in the house, including a dove, a lark, a dog and a parrot – which was kept as a reminder of her son who had been killed in action – that constantly squawked 'mother'. Despite the dirt, she was 'an awfully nice old woman, but very fond of breaking into tears'. If this accommodation left a lot to be desired, it was nothing compared to their next quarters, reached the following day near Fricourt – 'the camp is positively filthy, knee-deep in mud, bivvies very small and miserable. It has been raining all day so we are wet through'.

As October turned into November, Lidsey's probation with the Royal Flying Corps had yet to materialise, so it was life as usual with the Oxfordshires. The Battle of the Somme wore on, and the weather was awful, with near-constant rain. With resignation, on Thursday 2 November after their longest-ever spell in reserve, they left their mud-bound camp at 5.00 p.m. to proceed up to the line between Martinpuich and Le Sars, almost at the furthest point of the British advance on the Somme, to take over from the 6/7 Royal Scots Fusiliers. Things did not go well, though. After following a light railway for a short time, and then 'wandering about in a shell-devasted area' in mud up to their knees for almost three hours, the Royal Scots guide taking them to their trenches declared himself lost. A Company then blundered around in the dark for another hour trying to find their way, struggling through barbed-wire entanglements, a wood and artillery battery positions. Lidsey was furious, declaring himself 'at a loss to find words to express my feelings'. They eventually found a road to follow, but it was riddled with shell holes that were impossible to see since the road was under six inches of water and the night was pitch-black. Jack took over, 'prodding the road with my stick like a blind man', but the going was so slow that they barely made one mile per hour. Two of his men (or 'idiots', as he calls them) 'not having sense enough to follow the man in front of them' wandered into water-filled shell holes and 'disappeared up to their armpits in thick, liquid mud, and we had difficulty in getting them out; it was very lucky they were not drowned, although it would have been no loss. One of the two did it twice, and the other three times.' Eventually, just before midnight and after almost seven hours of wading about in miserable and filthy conditions, the exhausted men arrived at their destination, a reserve trench known as 26th Avenue on the forward slope of a hill in front of Bazentin, overlooking the Bapaume Ridge. Plastered in mud from head to foot, Jack and his men were dismayed to find that their new home was 'perfectly beastly; 6 inches deep in water with no accommodation for the men whatever; they, poor beggars, just had to sit down and sleep where they could'. After so long in the rear area, the conditions came as quite a shock. Finding a dump of corduroy nearby, A Company set about attempting to improve its environment by boarding the floor of 26th Avenue, eventually making it 'quite habitable'.

When daylight arrived next morning, Lidsey noticed an unfamiliar shape a couple of hundred yards away. It was a British tank – the first he or his men had ever seen – and it appeared to be abandoned. Curiosity got the better of them and they went to inspect it, and managed to get inside.[100] They marvelled at the leviathan machine, hearing that it had driven the 'Hun' out of Martinpuich, and that their flight had not stopped until they reached Le Sars. Seven hundred prisoners had apparently been taken by the Royal Scots Fusiliers, who had received only slight casualties.

On 4 November, the Oxfords moved forward, up to the support trenches. Setting off on a moonless night, 'the blackest on record', with few landmarks and in a torrential downpour, finding their way proved difficult once more, with some companies going through 'extraordinary adventures and did not reach their positions for five hours'.[101] Lidsey's platoon waded in knee-deep mud for about a mile and endured an enemy barrage en route, only again to find their new trench half full of filth. Some men arrived bare-footed, their boots lost to the quagmire along the way.

The following morning, A Company relieved C Company in the fire trench, known as Chalk Trench, a short distance north of Le Sars shortly before all hell let loose. On the Oxfordshires' right, the British 50th Division launched a major attack on the Butte de Warlencourt, a formidable German strongpoint built on an ancient burial mound that overlooked Le Sars and the Albert to Bapaume road. The British had already tried several times to dislodge the Germans from the redoubt, but so far the attempts had been expensive failures. Today was to prove no different. Massed German machine-gun fire cut into the advancing British, who could barely manage walking pace through the thick mud. Troops of the Durham Light Infantry did manage to get on to the Butte, but enemy counter-attacks pushed them off later in the day. The Oxfordshires' trenches were shelled heavily by the enemy in retaliation, and two of Jack's men, one of whom he described as his 'best man', were wounded. In all, the attack on the Butte de Warlencourt on 5 November 1916 cost around 1,000 British casualties, to no avail. Of the assault, the commanding officer of the Durham Light Infantry's 9th Battalion, Lieutenant Colonel Roland Bradford VC, said:

> The results which would have been gained in the event of success were of doubtful value, and would hardly have been worth the loss which we would suffer. The Butte itself would have been of little use to us for the purposes of observation. But the Butte de Warlencourt had become an obsession. Everybody wanted it. It loomed large in the minds of the soldiers in the forward area and they attributed many of their misfortunes to it. The newspaper correspondents talked about 'that miniature Gibraltar'. So it had to be taken. It seems that the attack was one of those tempting, and unfortunately at one period frequent, local operations which are so costly, and which are rarely worthwhile. But perhaps that is only the narrow view of the Regimental Officer.[102]

The Butte remained in German hands until late February 1917. It was recaptured by them during the Spring Offensive of 1918, before falling to the British once again in August that year.

Chalk Trench proved to be as dangerous a location as any that the Oxfords had occupied thus far. The headquarters of A Company was in an old German dugout and in full view of the enemy 500 yards away. Sniper fire from the opposite side was constant, and getting to and from the dugout proved an extremely hazardous journey, as Jack remarked: 'From Company HQ we have to double across 100 yards of ground open to the sniper to get into the communication trench; it is an exceedingly unpleasant experience, trying to run in 6 inches of mud and being shot at all the way. He had seven shots at one whilst running across, and it was no joke; he managed to wound two men during the day. He is luckily for us a very bad shot.'

The rain continued the following day, as did the shelling from the German artillery. One enemy '5-9' shell hit Lidsey's dugout 'plumb on', extinguishing the candles and cracking the roof in several places. Showered with mud, soil and debris, Jack and the other occupants managed to crawl their way to safety, with Jack noting that he 'thought we were buried'. At dusk that evening, three German soldiers appeared out of the gloom and rain to surrender to the Oxfordshires, walking forward with their hands raised and shouting 'advance to the English' as they came. Checking them over, the British found that they belonged to the same regiment as had faced the Oxfordshires at Thiepval earlier in the battle, namely the 64th Guards Reserve Infantry Regiment, part of the 1st Guards Reserve Division. Although a reserve unit, the division was considered by Allied intelligence to be dependable, and willing to take losses to hold and defend the line. Lidsey noted that his captives 'were very good specimens; one had the Iron Cross and could speak French moderately well. When they were being evacuated, the man escorting them was hit by shrapnel. The Huns bolted with funk; they were caught by some RAMC[103] orderlies who made them carry a stretcher.'

On hearing of the prisoners, the Oxfordshires' CO sent a bottle of whisky to Jack and his men by way of congratulation. The gift was very welcome, even if Lidsey felt slightly guilty about accepting it because the Germans had simply walked in unbidden and had saved his platoon the risk of carrying out a raid on the enemy's trenches to seize a 'Hun' or two.

Overnight on 6–7 November, the Oxfordshires were relieved by the Buckinghamshires. It was a full, bright moon that night, giving the Germans a clear view of what was going on as the soldiers crossed the ridge. Enemy artillery opened up, bringing down a furious barrage on the British. 'It was about the hottest barrage I have ever been in; we were exceedingly lucky, only having three casualties in the Company',

Jack wrote. He helped carry one wounded man to safety after applying a tourniquet to his leg injury, but was then wounded himself, or 'done up', as he put it. Lidsey goes into no more detail about his injury, simply saying that he 'had to sit down and rest a while' while his men went on ahead. Between 5 and 7 November 1916, the Oxfordshires lost nine men killed.

The next few days were spent in the reserve and communication trenches. The weather improved, although their living conditions did not. Now back in the muck and filth of 26th Avenue, life may have seemed preferable in the front line. Being in reserve also did not protect them from the enemy; on 8 November the Germans shelled A Company's positions, wounding six men, including two from Jack's 3 Platoon. Respite came two days later in the form of the Royal Warwickshires. Pleased to hand over their sodden, stinking trenches to the newcomers, the Oxfordshires went to the rear, glad of a chance to rest and clean themselves up. By this time, Jack had not shaved for nine days, and had worn out '1 pair boots; 1 pair breeches; 1 pair pants; 1 pair puttees; 2 pairs socks; 1 tunic and numerous handkerchiefs; rather an expensive week'.

The better weather held for the most part of their rest period, and the men occupied themselves with improving trenches, dugouts and their general living situation. Still within range of German artillery, however, the shelling continued, particularly on 12 November when Lidsey's working party was attacked when coming back from trench repair duty. Fortunately, there were no casualties this time, but in the forward line the Warwicks took six killed and numerous wounded. News came through that Beaumont-Hamel (along with 66 enemy officers and 3,300 men) had finally been captured; it had been an objective for the first day of the Somme battle, back on 1 July.

The Oxfordshires' last night before going up to the line at Le Sars once more was on Tuesday 14 November, and the officers pulled out all the stops to make it a memorable one. The mess put on a 'sumptuous meal' after travelling twenty-five miles to Amiens (without authorisation) to buy, beg, steal and borrow food. The menu card that night read:

Martini Cocktails
Lobster (Fresh)

Beef Cutlets
Green Peas; Kidney Beans
Trifle
Gorgonzola Cheese
Dessert
Coffee and Liqueurs

Next morning it was business as usual, preparing to move to the front. Jack's luck was in, however, and he was told that along with five per cent of the company, he was to remain behind in Albert as the battalion rear party; he was 'agreeably surprised' at the news. Arriving in the town later that night, he found his billet in a large house, and had the best night's sleep he had had in some time. Lidsey spent the next few days in and around Albert and Amiens and, with not much work to be done, he made sure that he rested and dined well. He did not forget that his men were up at the front, though, and he 'spent a lot of money buying things to send to the lads in the line – Martini cocktails, lobster and chicken, amongst other things'. He had a pleasant surprise on 19 November when, while visiting the field cashier in Albert, he saw a column of fresh troops marching into the town. It was the 61st (2nd South Midland) Division, a second-line division that contained the 2/4 Oxfordshires, those who had originally volunteered for home service only, but now, with an influx of new recruits, had deployed overseas. Jack saw many old faces 'including Wayto, Barton,[104] Fowler and Shilton; later, the little party of us had a champagne dinner together at the Officers' café. It was a great treat to meet some of the old pals again.'

Jack was on hand to welcome his own men back when they left the trenches on 21 November, meeting them at Villa station (near Contalmasion) to help dish out hot soup as they marched, or rather staggered, in. They had had a rough time of it; Battalion HQ had been hit by German artillery on the 17th, killing Lieutenant Reginald Lake and Private Eaton from A Company. Further casualties were taken while in the trenches and also as they came out of the line and were making their way back, bringing the total killed in the battalion during that spell at the front to eleven. The weather had grown cold, with the first sharp frosts beginning to bite, and Lidsey was shocked to see the state of the men as they plodded wearily back in. They were, he said, 'absolutely tired out, positively beaten, by the mud and cold'. Most of them were asleep before their meal had finished being served. Conditions had been terrible, with no hot food, trenches again knee-deep in mud, and constant shelling from the other side. If there had been one shred of consolation, it was that the mud absorbed much of the explosive effect of the German shells, bringing the destructive area of a dreaded '5-9' down to just a few yards. More than once, a man caught by an explosion found himself flung on to the lip of the resulting crater with just minor injuries.[105]

The last few men who had been with the battalion from the start of the Oxfordshires' campaign back in March 1915 and who had not yet had any leave were now able to go home for a few days' respite: '[They] will never forget the gradual transition from the waist-deep mud of the front line at Le Sars, across the shelled wilderness at Martinpuich, then back along the hopeless desolation of Contalmaison to Albert; there to be finally speeded by shells from a long-range gun before their train got away and any idea could be entertained that leave was a real thing.'[106]

Jack Lidsey never went into the line with The Oxfordshire & Buckinghamshire Light Infantry again. That same day, his orders for the Royal Flying Corps arrived, telling him to report to RFC HQ at Hesdin 'as soon as convenient'. With the Battle of the Somme drawing to a close, the next chapter of Second Lieutenant Lidsey's war was about to begin.

Chapter Nine

No. 16 Squadron, Royal Flying Corps, 22 November – 31 December 1916

On Wednesday 22 November 1916, Jack Lidsey bade farewell to his fellow officers and the men of A Company, 1/4 (Oxfordshire) Battalion. It must have been a wrench for him, leaving behind close friendships that had been forged in battle. He had been through so much with his comrades, joining up right at the start of the war, through the battles of 1915, and then the inferno that was the Somme in 1916. The battalion CO, Lieutenant Colonel Bartlett, told him that he was sorry to lose him; Bartlett could probably ill afford to part with such an experienced junior officer. Lidsey left his comrades at 11.00 a.m. and walked into Albert, from where he caught a train to Amiens. Here he bumped into another officer, Second Lieutenant Arthur Perryman of the Middlesex Regiment, who had also transferred to the Royal Flying Corps. The two aspiring aviators struck up an immediate friendship and made their way to Hesdin together, arriving at RFC HQ the next day after a protracted journey via Étaples. Interviewed by a colonel, Jack was ordered to report to HQ 1 Wing RFC at Chocques, from where he would be allocated to a front-line squadron.

At this stage of the RFC's existence, training for observers was at best somewhat haphazard. Those joining up directly in England were sent to one of the RFC's schools of military aeronautics, either Number 1 School in Reading, or Number 2 School in Oxford, where they would study the basics of map reading, gunnery and mechanics, before going on to the RFC Wireless School at Brooklands.[107] Following ground school, they were then posted to a home-based training squadron that was

working up to deployment to France, for flying experience and to put
their newly learned skills into practice. However, for those like Jack and
Arthur Perryman who were already serving in the Army in France, the
RFC saw little value in sending them home to be trained. Volunteers
simply arrived at their designated airfield, found their squadron, and got
into an aeroplane after being shown around it by the pilot – training
was very much 'on the hoof'. Many, like Lidsey, had never flown in an
aeroplane before, and had probably been no closer to one than watching
as it flew over their trench several hundred, if not thousands, of feet
above.

There was the odd lecture on artillery spotting or the Lewis Gun, and
arrangements were made to send novice observers and pilots to a Royal
Field Artillery gun battery for a few days to watch and learn about
gunnery procedure. Practice shoots were organised, with shells filled with
powder only (no explosives) produced for the purpose. Short courses
of a few days' duration were also held at artillery schools in France, but
that was about as far as ground instruction went, and in any case, such
tuition was given after joining a squadron, not before. As for training
manuals, the only one in circulation at the time was the 'RFC Notes for
Observers',[108] a sixty-three-page booklet published in June 1915 that
covered reconnaissance, cooperation of aeroplanes with other arms
(infantry and artillery) and offensive action. The appendices section
carried useful notes on such topics as the organisation of the RFC, and
the care and maintenance of the Lewis Gun. The manual became the new
observer's bible, although a notice in red lettering on the cover warned
that it was 'Not to be taken on reconnaissance'. There was, however, a
single-sided reconnaissance aide memoire,[109] hard-backed so that it could
be taken aloft, that covered the major features to watch out for while
airborne, such as columns of troops, artillery, transport and aerodromes.
The RFC had at least, though, identified the attributes that a probationer
required if he was to be awarded his observer badge after the relevant
experience in the air. A paper dated 29 July 1915 from HQ RFC to the
flying wings stated:[110]

Although it is undesirable to lay down any hard and fast rules as
regards the qualification of observers, it is considered that the same

general standard of proficiency should be maintained throughout the RFC. Normally, an officer should not be recommended for grading as a qualified observer unless:

a. He knows the Lewis Gun thoroughly
b. Can use the RFC camera successfully
c. Can send and receive by wireless at the rate of 6 words a minute with 98% accuracy
d. Knows the method of co-operation between aeroplanes and artillery thoroughly
e. Has carried out two reconnaissances or has ranged batteries successfully on two occasions.

By the time Jack Lidsey volunteered for flying duties, however, RFC HQ had reconsidered its reluctance to 'lay down hard and fast rules' regarding qualified observers. In a memorandum of 29 November 1916, formal examinations were introduced:[111]

Qualification of observers
These instructions are issued in order that the General standard of proficiency of observers may be improved and the degree of efficiency necessary for the qualifying of observers as trained observers may become more uniform.
An observer will be graded as a qualified observer on the recommendation of his Squadron Commander based on the results of the following tests:
Co-operation with artillery – Examiner: Wing Artillery Liaison Officer
Use and care of wireless – Examiner: Wing Wireless Officer
Photography and care of camera – Examiner: Brigade Photographic Officer
Use and care of machine guns – Examiner: Brigade Machine Gun Officer.

The appendices to the memorandum covered exactly what the examinee was expected to know within each subject, and the 'co-operation with artillery' section alone specified ten areas of competence. Award of the observer badge (a capital letter 'O' with a wing attached, earning it the derogatory nickname of 'the flying arsehole') was therefore far from automatic. Even with success in the exams, the recommendation of the squadron CO was still required, and such endorsement was not assured. Until they gained qualified status, probationary observers were on 'instructional pay' – a little over half that of their trained counterparts – a further incentive to make the grade.

After more experience, a qualified observer could apply to be selected for pilot training. For many, this had always been their aim, merely treating being an observer (often seen as coming a poor second to being a pilot) as a hurdle to be overcome on the way to a full set of 'wings'. There were financial inducements in addition to the kudos, since a pilot earned almost twice as much as a qualified observer. Furthermore, observers were often in limbo since they were classed as 'attached' to the RFC from their parent regiment and could not be permanently transferred until a vacancy arose (pilots were automatically transferred, however); this meant that, since they were neither part of their own unit nor on the full-time strength of the RFC, they were overlooked for promotion by both. Since an 'attached' observer could therefore not realistically expect to rise above the rank of lieutenant, the only ways to gain promotion were to learn to fly and become a pilot or, as happened in a number of cases, to ask to be returned to their regiment back in the trenches. The issue was addressed on 17 November 1916, when a report by a committee of inquiry into the administration of the RFC (instigated by the Government), the Bailhache Committee,[112] was published: 'We recommend that, during the war, and until our ideal of interchangeable observers and pilots is reached, observers should receive promotion without having to become pilots, and that a corps of observers be formed with a regular establishment graded for promotion among themselves.'

Unfortunately, though, the RFC was still slow to recognise the importance of observers, even with Bailhache's recommendations. One of the pilots with whom Jack was later to fly, Captain Davidson, said that 'the promotion of an observer to the rank of flight commander was more of a myth than a reality. It was, in fact, a rare occurrence.' Whether Lidsey had ambitions as a pilot, he makes no mention.

The commanding general of the RFC, Major General Sir Hugh

Trenchard (later acknowledged as the 'father' of the Royal Air Force), eventually recognised that fledgling observers joining from infantry regiments in France did need a proper programme of formal training. On 8 December 1916, he issued an order 'to send home Officers on joining the RFC on probation for a course of training as observers'.[113] Trenchard suggested a course lasting a month and laid down the subjects he wanted it to cover. His order stated that the time taken up with training observers by front-line squadrons could be better used, and that 'new observers often arrive in a squadron after a long spell in the trenches, without any leave, in an unfit condition to take up work demanding absolute freshness mentally and physically'. This unsatisfactory state of affairs certainly applied to Jack Lidsey, but he missed the new course by a little over a month; it was introduced in early January 1917.

Another delayed and interrupted journey by train eventually delivered Jack and Perryman to Chocques. During the train ride, Lidsey met a 'very nice young French lady' who spoke perfect English, having lived for a time in Northampton. They got on well, and when she left the train, she offered Jack an invitation to visit her at her home not far away in Bruay-la-Buissière. He 'very much hoped to see her again'.

No. 1 Wing HQ allocated both Lidsey and Perryman to No. 16 Squadron RFC, which was based near the young French woman's home at Bruay, some thirty miles south-west of Lille. The airfield was on the southern side of Bruay, a town built around the coal mining industry. There were four mines in the local area, and the town was dominated by the Bruay Mining Company, the chief local employer. Pyramid-like slag heaps from the pits loomed over the surrounding landscape, and the Western Front lay less than ten miles to the east.

No. 16 Squadron had been formed in February 1915 at the large RFC HQ aerodrome at nearby St Omer to carry out a mixture of offensive patrolling and reconnaissance duties, operating a combination of British and French aircraft types. The squadron was known as a 'corps squadron', reflecting its close cooperation duties with the ground Army. One of the squadron's early commanding officers was Major Hugh Dowding, who later masterminded RAF Fighter Command's victory in the Battle of Britain during the summer of 1940.

On Sunday 26 November 1916, Lidsey reported to the incumbent CO of No. 16 Squadron, Major Paul Maltby, and was sent to the squadron's 'B' Flight, which at the time was flying from a former French Army airfield at Savy-Berlette (also known as Savy-B, or just Savy), a short distance away to the south. Maltby had sent 'B' Flight to Savy as a liaison experiment since the airfield was closer to the artillery batteries with which the aircraft were working, and he felt that Bruay was 'very far back from the lines for a Corps squadron'.[114] It was at Savy that Jack Lidsey had his introduction to the Royal Aircraft Factory Bleriot Experimental 2, known more simply as the BE2, the aeroplane that was then operated by No. 16 Squadron.

The BE2 was a single-engined, two-seated tandem biplane, designed by Geoffrey de Havilland, that enjoyed an unenviable reputation within the RFC and was reviled by its crews. Entering service in 1912 in the light bomber and reconnaissance roles, the BE2 had performed well at the start of the war but was soon left behind by the pace of technological advance that the First World War heralded. By 1915, it was an outdated aircraft, having been designed before air-to-air combat had been envisaged, and was therefore easy prey for the new German types that were coming into service, especially the Fokker Eindecker. The Eindecker was the first purpose-built fighter aeroplane and featured a belt-fed machine gun synchronised to fire through the propeller, allowing for a far better aim at the target – wherever the aeroplane was pointing, the bullets would go in the same direction. This was a game-changer in the air war, as the RFC had no such technology at the time, and could only offer two inferior options. The first was to mount the engine and propeller behind the pilot in a 'pusher' configuration which, although offering an unobstructed arc of fire forwards, carried significant disadvantages in terms of structural complexity, centre of gravity, weight and drag, all of which made for a slow aeroplane. Second was the idea of armoured deflector plates attached to the propeller (on a conventionally mounted 'puller' engine in front of the pilot) that were supposed to protect the blades against being struck by the host aircraft's bullets, an innovation that did little to inspire confidence and could just as likely ricochet the pilot's own rounds back at him. British and French aircraft losses began to mount, leading to the so-called 'Fokker Scourge' during the latter part of 1915, and with the attrition came a surrender of air superiority over the Western Front to the Germans.

Because the term 'Fokker Scourge' was an invention of the British press, it was slightly misleading and sensationalist. Compared with the intense air fighting that took place in 1917 and 1918, the amount of Allied casualties during the 'Scourge' period was relatively small, partly due to the way that the Germans used Eindeckers, issuing them only in small numbers to existing reconnaissance squadrons – it was to be nearly another year before the Germans were to follow the British example of establishing specialist fighter squadrons. Also, there were fewer aeroplanes in use at the time, so the loss rate was logically smaller. Lastly, despite its advanced armament, the Eindecker was by no means an outstanding aircraft, but, nevertheless, the impact on Allied morale on the fact that the Germans were in control of the air created a major scandal in the British media.

There is no doubt about the psychological effect that the Eindecker's reputation had on the British aircrews. In his classic book *Sagittarius Rising*, RFC pilot Cecil Lewis said that: 'The Fokker was the menace of the RFC. Hearsay and a few lucky encounters had made the machine respected, not to say dreaded, by the slow, unwieldy machines then used by us for Artillery Observation and Offensive Patrols. Rumour credited it with the most fantastic performance! It could outclimb, outpace, and outmanoeuvre anything in the RFC. You were as good as dead if you as much as saw one, and so on. In short, our morale wanted bucking up.'[115]

Lewis flew a BE2c, along with examples of other Allied aircraft, against a captured Eindecker for comparison, and found that 'all of them gave quite a good account of themselves except the [BE]2c, which in performance, was nowhere.'[116]

The BE2's vulnerability to enemy fighters earned it the British nickname of 'Fokker Fodder'. To the Germans it was known, tellingly, as '*Kaltes Fleisch*' – cold meat. Even in 1916, in its latest, improved, E and F versions, the BE2 could only achieve around 90mph. By then the Germans were replacing the Eindecker with newer, even more advanced aircraft such as the Albatros D.III, which sported two synchronised machine guns and was capable of speeds of up to 110mph, against which the BE2 was virtually helpless. Such was the BE's dreadful performance that no less a person than the legendary British fighter ace Captain Albert Ball, VC,

called it 'a bloody awful aeroplane'. The best guidance that could be given
to a new BE2 pilot on what to do if attacked was summed up by No. 16
Squadron pilot and 'A' Flight commander Captain Eric Routh, who
said: 'When a new pilot reported to me my advice was 1: Ceaselessly search
the sky, however much you may trust your observer. 2: If a Hun gets
behind you, never dive away from him; feint, sideslip, anything you can
think of, but don't dive. 3: Look over your shoulder to see if he is getting
a lead on you; if he is, it is time to do something.'[117]

The strength of feeling about the BE2, and the state of British aircraft
manufacturing in general, was so great that the subject was raised in
a heated debate in the House of Commons in March 1916 when the
independent MP and former Royal Naval aviator, Noel Pemberton Billing,
sought to reform the leadership of the RFC and to end the monopoly of
the Royal Aircraft Factory's supply of aircraft to the military. In an
inflammatory speech to Parliament on 22 March, he opined that British
pilots were being 'rather murdered than killed' in France because of the
BE2's poor performance and called it a 'travesty of a weapon of war'.
The Conservative MP for Brentford, William Joynson-Hicks, rallied to
Pemberton Billing's cause, telling the House a few weeks later:

I myself have been out to the front and seen the organisation of our
Air Service there. I saw any number of new machines, all of the same
old type of machines that we used when the War began, with the
same old engines of eighty-five, ninety, and ninety-five horsepower.
What I have been trying to impress, time and time again, is that you
cannot meet a German machine of 150 horse-power with an English
machine of 90 or 95 horse-power. That is my whole case against the
Flying Corps, as I told the right hon. Gentleman in private conference some time ago. What I want is to have someone in charge of
the Air Service who will stop the making of these machines. My
right hon. Friend knows that a contract was given a little time ago
to an English firm for 1,000 90 horsepower engines. They are being
pressed for delivery still. Why is not that contract scrapped at once
and a new contract entered into, not for 95 horse-power machines,
but for 200 horse-power machines? I know that there are other
higher horse-power machines being built, but what is the good of

turning out 1,000 engines of 95 or 90 horse-power? Up till now our machines have been maids-of-all-work. They have had to carry a pilot, an observer, one or two guns, ammunition, a few bombs here and there, photographic apparatus, and wireless equipment. No wonder they are called Christmas Trees at the front. They are decked all over with all kinds of these things, and they cannot go more than the certain number of miles per hour they went at the beginning of the War. I have no time to describe them. My right hon. Friend knows the types of machines we must have if we are to win the battle in the air.[118]

Warming to his theme, Joynson-Hicks read out part of a letter he had received from 'a captain in the Flying Corps':

He says: 'At the front the tales you are told about our mastery of the air are known by all of us out here to be absolutely incorrect. We have not got the mastery. We have the pluck, we have not got the machines. It may soothe the British public's mind, but we airmen know the truth.' That is not a satisfactory position. That is not really a position in which we ought to put our men, gallant as they are. This man is a gallant man and is a Military Cross officer.[119]

The two MPs made compelling, if controversial (and in the case of Pemberton Billing, self-serving, since he owned an aircraft manufacturing business), arguments, and their speeches led to the formation by the Government of the Bailhache Committee (chaired by Sir Clement Bailhache, a high court judge) referred to above. However, the long development times involved in designing, building, and testing new aircraft meant that, for now, the BE2 would remain in RFC service, and in large numbers.

Aside from its slow speed, there were other reasons why the BE2 was so unloved. First, the pilot sat in the rear seat so that the machine's centre of gravity would not be unduly disturbed if it was being flown solo, thus placing the observer in the front cockpit, which was directly over, and between, the wings. This meant that the wings, struts and bracing wires that surrounded the observer, and the engine directly in front of him, restricted his field of view (the best sight he could get was slightly forwards and straight down, due to the stagger of the lower wing) and hampered the operation of the camera and/or the Lewis Gun (for self-defence) – hardly ideal for an 'observer'.

Secondly, since the BE2 had been designed before the war, no consideration had been given to arming it for self-protection and, in any case, in its early versions, the aeroplane's engine was not powerful enough to cope with the additional weight of a gun, ammunition and mounts. As the war progressed and improved engines were introduced, front-line squadrons began to experiment with 'home-made' solutions for mounting a Lewis Gun. These ad-hoc designs were later adopted officially but, even in modified form, were still far from ideal. The observer's Lewis Gun was able to be mounted in only one of three positions at a time: one on each of the forward centre-section struts to either side of his cockpit, and one behind him, between his and the pilot's cockpits (known as the Strange Mount after its inventor, Captain L. Strange). If the arc of fire needed changing, the observer had to stand up, lift the twenty-eight-pound weapon off its swivel mount and heave it from one position to the next – not easy in flight while under attack, and when the BE2 was manoeuvring. If the marauding fighter was coming in from behind, which was usually the case following the introduction of the Eindecker, it meant firing rearwards over the pilot's head (using the Strange Mount) while kneeling on the front seat. Another Lewis Gun could be mounted either in a fixed position alongside the pilot's cockpit on the fuselage (angled outwards at forty degrees to prevent it shooting off the propeller), or to swivel mounts on the rear centre-section struts in front of the pilot. Aiming and operating this second weapon, especially changing the ninety-seven-round magazine,[120] meant that the pilot's attention was distracted from actually flying the aeroplane, so it was usually only carried when the pilot flew alone.

Thirdly, the aerodynamic design of the BE2 led to problems. Competing theories on aeroplane design in 1912 held that either an aircraft should be built as inherently *unstable*, meaning that the airframe will naturally deviate from straight and level flight and must be brought back to steadiness by corrections from the pilot, or inherently *stable* so that any movement away from straight and level must be initiated, rather than corrected, by the pilot. The unstable aeroplane will therefore be more manoeuvrable, but will be trickier to fly, than the more forgiving (but less agile), stable design. The BE2 was built to be stable, hardly surprising given the inexperience of pilots and the paucity of flying training in those early years of manned flight. It was so steady that it could be flown for long periods (in good weather) without the pilot touching the control column and would right itself if upset by a sudden gust of wind. Such gentle manners were so unusual in early aeroplanes that pilots called the BE2 'Stability Jane', or 'The Quirk'. Stability also made the BE2 a very good platform for observation and photography, which is what it was designed for, but of course this did not help it under dogfight conditions when agility was the key to survival.

It was towards one of these outdated, underperforming machines that Jack Lidsey walked on the early afternoon of 26 November 1916 for his first experience of flying. The weather was not good, and very little flying had taken place anywhere over the Western Front all day, but the need to blood a new observer was pressing. Having been designed for observation, the BE2 positioned its crew in open cockpits with their heads and shoulders above the level of the fuselage to give them the best possible view, but in so doing exposing them to the biting blast of the slipstream and the –two- to three-degree Celsius drop in air temperature for every 1,000 feet of altitude gained. Wearing the correct clothing was therefore of prime importance, as stressed by the 'RFC Notes for Observers' booklet: 'It is essential that observers should be warmly clad before starting on reconnaissance. The extra clothing worn may be uncomfortable on the ground, but it is not superfluous when travelling at 60 or 70 miles per hour at 6.000 feet.'[121] Taking the advice given in the preamble to the booklet on how to dress for flying, Lidsey would have swaddled himself against the late autumn chill in a leather flying helmet over a balaclava; goggles; thigh-length sheepskin-lined flying boots; a wool-lined long leather coat over his uniform, woollen waistcoat and long johns; leather gauntlets over woollen gloves; and perhaps his old Magdalen College School scarf knotted around his neck. The booklet also helpfully suggested that Vaseline was 'useful for the hands and feet as a protection against the cold'.

Jack was shown around the aeroplane by his pilot, Second Lieutenant

Rodney Franklin (an Australian, known by his middle name, Vernon, and a veteran of the ill-fated Gallipoli landings of 1915 before he became a pilot), who pointed out the important parts and showed Lidsey how to clamber into the cramped front cockpit of the BE2c (serial number 4592, built under licence by the Scottish engineering firm G. & J. Weir Ltd), also telling him what to touch, and what not to touch. As he settled himself into his seat and strapped himself in, Jack could not have failed to notice that the main fuel tank sat less than an arm's length directly in front of him, level with his face and chest. The secondary petrol tank was behind him, between him and the pilot – he was sandwiched between the two highly inflammable areas.

In the days before electric starters, coaxing the aeroplane's engine into life was a risky, manual process. If the procedure was not adhered to, it could mean dismemberment, or worse, for the mechanic detailed to start the aircraft's motor. Franklin would have given the airman standing by the propeller a thumbs-up to show that he was ready to begin. The mechanic would return the gesture before grasping one of the BE2's four propeller blades and shouting 'Switches off; petrol on' to Franklin, who would make sure that the magneto switches in his cockpit were off (thereby ensuring that the engine would not start prematurely) before he responded with the same words – 'Switches off; petrol on'. Thus reassured, the airman would shout 'Air closed – sucking in', before turning the propeller a couple of times to draw fuel into the carburettors to prime them. When he was satisfied, he would then call 'Switch on' to Franklin. The magneto switches would be returned to their 'on' positions, and the pilot would have shouted 'Switches on' by way of confirmation. One last yell from the mechanic – 'Contact' – before he gave the propeller a heave, and the engine would then, hopefully, catch and come alive. Once Franklin was happy that his gauges were showing that the motor was performing correctly, he would have waved the chocks away from the main wheels before a short taxy out on to the grass and turning into wind, a roar as the engine built up revolutions, a few bumps as they increased speed, and then … airborne.

As they climbed, Franklin swung the machine eastwards towards Arras and the front line – a first look at the trenches from above for Jack. The Germans were not going to allow this to be a joyride, though, and sent a single round of 'Archie' – anti-aircraft fire – towards them, as if by way of welcoming Lidsey to the game. Afterwards, Franklin 'tried to put the wind up me by doing spirals etc; glorious sensation, flying in a BE biplane'. They touched down forty-five minutes later, having only reached a maximum altitude of 2,000 feet due to low cloud. If Lidsey enjoyed his first trip, then things got even better that night when he moved into his billet in a house close to the airfield, which he described as 'average', but noted that, for the infantry, it would be considered as 'excellent'. The Royal Air Force of today has obviously inherited its penchant for decent accommodation from its RFC forebears.

Sightseeing was all well and good, but Lidsey was there to work. With training being done on the job, his next flight the following day was to register the fall of shot for a battery of British 18-pounder artillery pieces. Artillery observation was bread and butter to the RFC corps squadrons and a boon to the gunners. The advent of air power ushered in the ability to see deep into enemy territory, meaning that the aircrew could watch to see where the guns' shells were landing. Then, by using a simple 'clock-ray' method, the aircraft's observer would report back to the battery with Morse code instructions on what aiming corrections to make until the target was successfully engaged. It was hazardous work, however – spotting for artillery made the aeroplane a prime target for the enemy, both his anti-aircraft gunners and his fighter pilots (in the latter case, the more so since aircraft on artillery observation tasks were, more often than not, unescorted). Blinding the guns was an excellent way of stopping them from shooting at you. Good artillery observation required skill and practice, but the lack of training made for often mixed results as inexperienced observers frequently called shoots as successful that, in reality, were not, and there could well have been a feeling that 'close enough is good enough' when the aircraft was a sitting target for the enemy and the imperative was to get away as quickly as possible.

And then there were wireless failures, bad positioning, misunderstood signals and a host of other potential complications to be dealt with. Above all, though, was the threat from German fighters. Eric Routh wrote:[122] 'When on artillery spotting, we had no direct fighter protection. If your observer did not keep awake, your first intimation of trouble would be a warning round from our own AA [anti-aircraft guns] or the very nasty 'rat-a-tat-tat' of the Hun machine gun. I developed a rubber neck whilst on that job. It was essential. Those that did not possess that commodity paid the highest penalty.'

Lidsey and Vernon Franklin took off at 1.25 p.m. and headed for the front line for what proved to be an eventful sortie: 'We received a hot strafe from machine guns in the trenches. Two bullets pierced the body just in the rear of the pilot's seat. Was up for 1 hr 25 mins; was nearly frozen when we came down as I had no flying boots on. Air pressure on ears after landing very painful – did not notice it yesterday.' His ear problems were probably due to the altitude on this flight, 4,000 feet, double that of the previous day.

The next few days brought 'dud' weather, mainly due to fog, which meant no flying. Jack used the time productively, learning wireless procedure and the principles of artillery spotting. Major Maltby was a stickler for Morse code proficiency and insisted that his observers were able to send sixteen words per minute during training on the ground so that they could work at a rate of twelve words a minute in the more challenging environment of the air. This meant that 'their messages took a shorter time to send with the result that the chances of jambing [sic] were reduced, and they were able to observe an appreciably larger number of [artillery] rounds during one flight'.[123] Maltby examined and critiqued the wireless log from every sortie personally, and then had it scrutinised by the squadron wireless officer from a technical perspective before it was passed back to the officer who had originated it. Woe betide any observer who did not come up to the CO's exacting standards.

Orders came through that 'B' Flight was to return to Bruay to rejoin the rest of No. 16 Squadron since the Savy experiment had 'proved un-economical'.[124] After dismantling the hangars and huts for transportation by lorry, Lidsey and the other observers also went by road on 29 November, but bad weather meant that the pilots had to wait to fly the BE2s back the next day. The weather was still marginal, meaning that they made the trip at barely 200 feet. The poor meteorological conditions continued, with each new day being greeted with 'pea soup' fog and sharp frosts. Jack continued his studies, both theory and practical. He mastered the C-Type reconnaissance camera and honed his skill with the Lewis Gun on the firing range.

It was a week before the weather cleared sufficiently to allow Jack to fly again, on Monday 4 December 1916. The sortie was another artillery observation with Franklin, but it proved to be a wasted journey since the gunners were not answering Jack's wireless signals, and they returned to Bruay at 11.36 a.m. after an hour in the air. No rest for the wicked, though – the pair were airborne once more at 12.10 p.m. to try again. If Jack thought that his flight on 27 November was 'hot', then this sortie was about to prove positively boiling. Some fifty minutes after take-off, they were at 7,500 feet above Bailleul-Sir-Berthoult when:

The 'archies' came up and barked at us like a big dog, but did not get dangerously close. Three Huns then attacked us; one dived at us and opened up with his machine gun. I got to my Lewis Gun and waited for him, holding my fire as I did not consider him close enough. Two FE8s [125] came to our assistance; had they not been there, we must surely have gone under. They brought one of the Huns down, his right wing falling off when about 1,000ft from the ground, he went right into the ground nose-first. Went back over the lines to wind our aerial up[126] and returned to see if we could help the FE8s. There were however no Huns to be seen, so we just hovered about for a time. Saw a Hun some way below us, so dived on him and gave him a drum of the best. He showed us his tail very quickly.

Safely back on the ground, they compiled their formal combat report for the sortie, stating that the attack was by three Roland aircraft, which had come in from behind:

The observer could not get his gun on them, so turned to use the front mounting, but they were then 800 to 1,000 feet above us. At this time two FE8s joined us and brought one enemy machine down. It crashed (after one wing had folded up) near Bailleul. When near Avion at 7,000 feet saw another enemy machine below us over Mericourt. Immediately dived and fired one drum from the front mounting. The hostile aircraft turned and went slowly in the direction of Henin Lietard.[127]

In fact, two of the Germans had been shot down, and the enemy aircraft were not Rolands as they had thought but were Albatros fighters of *Jasta 12*.[128] The British FE8s were from No. 40 Squadron; Captain Dennis Mulholland[129] and Lieutenant Edwin Benbow[130] were on patrol when they saw three hostile aeroplanes manoeuvring for position to assault the lone BE2. Mulholland attacked and destroyed one of the German machines (probably the one that Lidsey and Franklin saw go down), piloted by *Vizefeldwebel*[131] Wilhelm Hennebeil, while Benbow got to within fifty feet of a second enemy aircraft and fired twenty rounds, seeing it turn over and fall to earth in a slow, spinning nose dive.[132]

Once again, Lidsey and Franklin had brought home a machine 'damaged by MG fire'. They had been extremely fortunate that the British fighters had seen them and come to their rescue, since three to one against were not survivable odds, particularly in a BE2. If Jack was feeling pleased with himself after his first aerial combat, Franklin certainly did not share his elation – he tore into Lidsey for not opening fire with the Lewis Gun, even if Jack had felt that the range was too great. In what was probably a very one-way conversation liberally sprinkled with Antipodean profanity, Franklin 'informed' Lidsey that they 'were very lucky to be alive'. Eric Routh summarised the fire-or-wait predicament thus: 'It is absolutely imperative that the observer should not be surprised; alas it is not advisable in a BE2 to withhold your fire on the chance of bringing him [the enemy] down. If you fire at him when at 500 yards your chances of putting him off his aim are much better; also the cone of fire will be much larger and one or two of the shots may go close to him and may have the desired effect.'[133]

The winter weather closed in again. Unlike in the trenches, if the weather was bad then there was not much to do on a flying unit, so Lidsey concentrated on his studies again and was examined in photography by the No. 1 Wing photography officer on 10 December, passing successfully. That evening, after a game of football against No. 1 Brigade RFC HQ (4–0 to No. 16 Squadron), he and some of his squadron comrades went to a concert in aid of the French Red Cross. Jack described the performance as 'first rate. The star turns were Mme Vaucaire (Paris), and Captain Marshall and the Very Lights (Canadians). The proceeds amounted to 1,000 Francs.'

Flying was possible the next morning, and for the second time Jack Lidsey found himself locking horns with the enemy in the air: 'Left the ground at 7.40am with Lt Marshall on counter-battery patrol[134]. Saw numerous trains, barges, and two balloons. Saw a Hun over our lines and proceeded to attack him. Before we could get to him, however, two FEs got to him and brought him down. Returned to aerodrome 9.10am; no flying after midday, more rain.'

There is no record of a German aircraft being shot down by FE8s on 11 December 1916. The official RFC communiqué for that day nevertheless states that 'an FE8, attacked by two hostile machines, had its petrol tank shot through, and on the return journey to the lines, an ammunition drum flew out of the [stowage] pocket and hit the propeller. The hostile machines were eventually driven off by a BE2.'[135] It is highly likely that it was Lidsey and Marshall who saved the FE8 from a worse fate.

The rain turned to snow and for the next few days not much flying happened. Even when aviation was possible, more often than not low cloud made observation difficult and sorties were curtailed. Flying with Lieutenant Harry Bagot on 13 December, Lidsey was tasked to do an artillery shoot, but the weather was so poor that the cloud base was down to 600 feet and they were forced to stop. On their way back to Bruay, the trailing aerial would not wind back in – the cable drum was probably frozen – so they had to break the wire and let it fall to earth.

On 16 December one of Lidsey's squadron comrades, Lieutenant J.P. Greenwood, returned from a sortie having been hit at 2,500 feet by a bullet from a German machine gun in the trenches. The round had shattered his right knee and severed an artery; with typical British understatement, Jack described it as a 'rather nasty wound'.

The weather continued to bring frustration. Jack flew with his flight commander, Captain Leask, on the afternoon of the 19th, on a counter-battery patrol. They were back just twenty-five minutes later, 'hopelessly dud, gale blowing, clouds at 500 feet and thick ground mist'.

Lidsey put his new-found skill of aerial photography into practice for the first time on 20 December. Getting airborne at 10.55 a.m. with Marshall once again at the controls, they returned after twenty minutes with Marshall 'feeling ill'. They went off again at 12.10, with Marshall evidently recovered from whatever was wrong with him, and headed over the German lines to image enemy positions. Once again, the Germans gave the British fliers a warm reception:

> Received a good peppering from 'archies', they were uncomfortably close, bursting in fours. Had a bullet through our plane at 6,000ft from the trenches. We were attacked by a Roland, who dived on our tail, gave him a drum from the rear mounting before he opened fire [Jack had obviously learned his lesson about opening fire regardless of the range]; he did a double turn and cleared off to his own lines at his best pace. Did not have the luck to bring him down but must have hit him several times. Exposed 18 plates,[136] most of which were a success. Returned to aerodrome at 1.40. Very sharp frost.

Strong winds and torrential rain led No. 16 Squadron into the run-up to Christmas, once more curtailing the prospects of flying. Christmas Eve bought a brief respite in the weather, and Jack found himself getting off the ground in the early afternoon, this time with Captain Leask at the controls, on an artillery observation sortie. Five minutes later, they were back at Bruay with a broken wireless. The squadron wireless technicians tinkered with the set briefly and then declared it serviceable, so Leask and Lidsey took off again a few minutes later. In the freezing December air, Jack tried for an hour to get a response from the gun battery, but with no success – his wireless set still refused to work. On the ground, angry and stiff with cold, the airmen vented their frustration on the wireless men.

Christmas Day 1916 dawned 'gloriously dud' at Bruay, making flying impossible, which no doubt came as a great relief to the 'three poor pilots' who had been ordered to carry out a bombing raid early on Christmas morning. The pilots and observers spent the day quietly, opening letters and parcels from home and catching up on some much-needed sleep. Come Christmas night, however, the relaxed atmosphere disappeared in Jack's billet:

> 7pm saw the commencement of some dinner, to which eleven of us sat down. Nothing was left of a 21lb turkey, plumb[sic] pudding flaming with brandy (for which occasion the lights were put out), a dozen bottles of champagne, and heaps of other little dainties.

A highly successful dinner for which we have to thank Madame (the landlady) who did the cooking. We then went round to the men's concert; found them making awful fools of themselves, disgustingly drunk. It was an excellent concert. An exceedingly drunk 'poilu'[137] who came in from no-one knows where, caused a great deal of amusement by trying to embrace and kiss all the officers, one of whom, more inebriated than the rest of his Flight, embraced the Frenchie on the stage. We retired at 11.30, to let the men go as they liked.

Nursing a sore head on Boxing Day, Jack received the sad news of the sudden death of his grandmother a few days earlier.

The weather, and presumably the various hangovers around the squadron, had cleared sufficiently to allow for flying on 27 December. Perhaps the Germans were also suffering the after-effects of a riotous Christmas since Jack flew twice that day, noting 'very pleasant flight[s]; no archies, no Huns, no MGs from trenches'.

Jack saw out the remaining days of 1916 on a three-day course at the 1st Army Artillery School, which was based at nearby Aire. The aim of the course was to educate him, as a tyro observer, in the ways and means of gunnery. Lectures included details about the different types of guns, their mechanisms, and their relative capabilities and effectiveness. One lesson that he found 'very good' was on air-to-ground liaison, vital for his observer role. Jack enjoyed the course and found it of immense value but felt that it was far too short. Armed with new, if scant, knowledge he headed back to Bruay, stopping along the way at St Omer where he 'spent an enjoyable afternoon and also a lot of money. Returned to the Squadron with a tender full of goods.'

The year 1916 had been an eventful one for Jack Lidsey. Following commissioning, the horror of the protracted Battle of the Somme had given way to his new-found career as an aviator. He had survived both, and he was perhaps looking forward to the new year and whatever challenges it might bring.

Chapter Ten

No. 16 Squadron, Royal Flying Corps,
1 January – 28 February 1917

The new year was seen in with a game of football against No. 10 Kite
Balloon Section, which No. 16 Squadron won easily, 7–0, and an
examination on the subject of artillery that Jack passed successfully –
hardly surprising given his attendance on the artillery course the week
before.

Tuesday 2 January brought Lidsey the first brush with disaster of
1917. Leaving the ground at 2.45p.m. for a contact patrol[138] with Lieutenant
Percival Murray as the pilot, the BE2's engine cut out almost immediately.
Engine failure was a regular occurrence with early aeroplanes and one
of the most hazardous emergencies to deal with, particularly on take-
off when the machine had very little airspeed and no altitude to spare,
and was in a nose-high attitude. All too often the aircraft would stall
and dive into the ground, with predictable consequences for the crew.
This time, fortunately, Murray 'just managed' to coax the ailing BE2 back
to the airfield, no mean accomplishment considering they had barely
reached 200 feet of altitude when the engine stopped.

The first week of the year brought decent flying weather, and Jack
made several trips with different pilots, including Leask, Bagot and
Marshall, on a variety of tasks including artillery spotting, photo
reconnaissance and contact patrols, all of which appear to have been
successful and with no major disruptions by the enemy. On 5 January,
No. 16 Squadron carried out a bombing raid on German positions at
Fournès, some nine miles beyond the front line, as part of a major
bombing operation carried out by several squadrons of No. 1 Brigade

RFC (to which No. 16 Squadron was subordinated). Observers were generally not carried on such sorties to compensate for the weight of the bombs, so Jack stayed behind. Several of the British aircraft were hit by anti-aircraft fire, but all returned to Bruay safely and with no casualties.

Having missed the raid on Fournès, Lidsey next flew on the 7th, a successful artillery shoot with Lieutenant Vernon Stewart as his pilot. Taking off at 8.20 a.m., they were up for two and a half hours, returning stiff with cold 'and jolly hungry, had breakfast at mid-day'. Once fed, they drove to visit the gun battery with whom they had been working, but 'got lost somewhere near the line, beyond Mount St Eloy [sic – actually Mont-Saint-Éloi]. Waded about in mud for some considerable time, where Stewart lost a shoe.' With his unfortunate companion no doubt cursing while hopping about trying to keep out of the worst of the mud, Jack eventually found the battery. Darkness had settled on Bruay by the time they made it back to the airfield, where they learned that 'during the day five machines were damaged by Archies, three of which were absolutely riddled. A piece of shell stuck in one observer's belt.'

On the morning of 11 January, the Germans decided to return the compliment for the Fournès raid of the 5th. At 3.00 a.m., No. 16 Squadron had a rude awakening:

Mr Hun sent umpteen machines over to bomb our aerodrome; he made a very successful show of it, dropping fourteen bombs on the aerodrome. One fell in C Flight hangar, set it on fire and burned five machines to cinders. There were only five casualties, including Sgt Drew (a pilot) who was hit by a piece of one of our own bombs – which was attached to one of the machines on fire – whilst he was on top of the adjoining hangar, preventing sparks from setting that alight too. When he was hit he was blown off the top of the hangar on to the ground – about 20 feet fall. I lay in my bed the whole time and heard the bombs bursting 50 yards from the house. Did not think it was so close to the aerodrome, or should have got up; as it was, I missed no end of fun.

Sergeant Drew was part of a firefighting party that was attempting – successfully – to stop the inferno in 'C' Flight's hangar spreading to the adjacent 'A' Flight hangar. The other casualties included a mechanic named Best who had been sleeping in the 'C' Flight hangar when it was hit and was wounded in the leg by a bomb splinter, and another, Callaghan, who was hit by a bomb fragment in the hand as he was fighting the fire.[139] As quickly as it had started, the raid was over – there had not even been time to man the airfield's anti-aircraft machine-gun pits before the attackers made off. In terms of human casualties, No. 16 Squadron had got off lightly, but in addition to the wrecked aircraft and hangar, significant damage had been done to precious wireless equipment, vehicles, tools and spares. This deadly game of tit for tat continued when 'within an hour of when the Huns bombed us, we went over and had set fire to one of their hangars on Douai aerodrome'.

Jack successfully passed his wireless examination later that day, the last test on the official syllabus, meaning that his name was now able to be put forward for fully qualified observer status, or 'flying officer observer', as it was called. As his experience increased, so did his squadron responsibilities; on 13 January he was told that he was 'now to be trained as an equipment officer. Heaps more work to do and tons to learn. Started today learning engines and indent forms etc. Shall now have my time fully occupied every dud day.'

Lidsey and Percival Murray were involved in another close shave due to mechanical problems with their aircraft, this time on 15 January. For some reason, on take-off the BE2 refused to gain airspeed and barely made it into the air, just managing to clear the road at the airfield's perimeter. Fortunately, there was no traffic otherwise they would surely have hit it. Once they had struggled into the cold January air, they lost sight of the ground at around 1,500 feet due to mist suddenly forming. Then, the aircraft continually turned to the left of its own accord due to being incorrectly rigged; Murray would have needed to keep constant opposite pressure on the rudder and stick just to keep the machine flying in a straight line. Next, the engine throttle decided to jam open, and then, as if they did not have enough to cope with, their aerial cable spool stuck fast, with the wire cable trailing along behind the aircraft. Any one of these problems was serious enough on its own, but a combination of them was distinctly life-threatening. Murray and Lidsey must have been wondering how, or indeed if, they would make it make to Bruay –

or anywhere at all for that matter – safely.

To round the situation off, Murray's agitated hand signals told Jack that he was lost. Fortunately, while Murray had been wrestling with the controls, Lidsey was able to do little to help other than look over the sides of the fuselage and keep an eye on where they were whenever the mist thinned enough to see the ground. In a magnificent feat of airmanship, Murray miraculously managed to land an aeroplane that wanted to go in its own direction, which was trailing a length of aerial cable that threatened to snag around the airframe or trees as they descended, while barely able to see the ground, *and* unable to control the engine. Jack told his diary that he was 'jolly thankful to find myself on the ground safely again'. After such a petrifying experience, it must have come as a relief to Lidsey that the next few days brought the first winter snow, making flying impossible.

The weather kept No. 16 Squadron on the ground until 21 January, when Jack and Vernon Stewart headed off to do artillery observation with the Royal Garrison Artillery's No. 68 Siege Battery, a heavy howitzer unit. The task was called off owing to bad visibility, but on the way back to Bruay, Lidsey spotted two British artillery batteries in the open, with no camouflage, and therefore vulnerable to enemy counter-battery fire. After landing, the two airmen jumped into one of the squadron's lorries and motored around to where they had seen the guns and explained their conspicuousness to the battery commander.

Later that afternoon, a German aircraft flew low around the Bruay area, firing coloured flares as it went. Intrigued, Lidsey and his comrades watched as the enemy aircraft descended, not in any obvious trouble but looking like he was going to land. Sensing good sport, No. 16 Squadron's pilots and observers piled into one of the squadron tenders and set off in hot pursuit of the 'Hun', craning their necks to see where the plane might come down as the truck careered along the local roads. A few miles further on, the German aircraft landed at 'B' Flight's old airfield of Savy-B. As the British truck swerved to a halt, its occupants leaped off in time to see the enemy fliers burning their machine, and then set about each other with flailing fists and feet: 'The pilot (an NCO) and the observer (an officer) then had a jolly good fight, kicking each other and scrapping furiously. The observer was probably "giving it" to the pilot for getting lost. He had been sent up to take photos over the Somme area – his compass failed to work, and he got lost.' The German aircraft was a Rumpler, a reconnaissance machine. It had apparently landed so that the observer, *Leutenant* Walter Hermann, could get his bearings. Hermann had left the aircraft to check his map, when the pilot, *Vizefeldwebel* Alexander Thurau, noticed British troops close by. Thurau decided to take off and make a break for home (thereby leaving Hermann to be captured) but saw RFC fighters taking off, so he surrendered instead, but not before destroying the Rumpler. The bemused British let the two enemy airmen get on with their fight until the military police arrived and escorted the prisoners away, presumably still bickering about who was to blame for their predicament.

The following day, Lidsey took off at 11.00 a.m. with Lieutenant Fred Gay at the controls to do a shoot with No. 161 Siege Battery, a unit operating huge 9.2-inch howitzers to obliterate enemy trenches by dropping high-explosive shells each weighing 290lb on a steep trajectory. It was bitterly cold, and once they had arrived on-station at 1,500 feet, they had to fly around in circles, getting colder and colder, because the battery was not ready to fire and had signalled the aeroplane to 'wait for 20 minutes'. Whilse they were circling, the BE2's engine began to misfire and the visibility dropped to dangerously low levels, so Gay decided to end the sortie and go home. They flew through two snowstorms on the way back, getting lost in the process and all the while nursing the stuttering engine. Jack fortunately managed to work out where they were, and they landed back at Bruay some seventy-five minutes after taking off, cold to the core and fortunate to be back in one piece.

Jack Lidsey had now been with No. 16 Squadron for two months, and probably considered himself to be an old hand. In terms of the life expectancy of RFC crews, he perhaps was not far wrong. On 23 January, he went aloft with Lieutenant Morris, 'a new pilot, the first time he had seen the lines', on another artillery observation task. The sortie ended prematurely after the trailing wireless aerial became entangled in their tail skid, meaning that maintaining contact with the gunners was impossible. Just as well, since they saw seven hostile aircraft, but 'luckily for us, none of them had the offensive spirit' – Jack probably would not have wanted to tangle with the enemy with a novice pilot at the controls of the BE2. That afternoon, Lidsey noted, the RFC 'lost an FE8 and an FE2b; they [the enemy] will have to pay for this tomorrow.'[140]

With better weather in late January, No. 16 Squadron became busier. As the snow cleared, artillery observation became a regular occurrence. On the 24th, Jack was again spotting for No. 161 Siege Battery. The guns fired sixty rounds during the shoot, of which five destroyed around 100 yards of enemy trench. Next day, the same task, but this time working with No. 6 Canadian Siege Battery. Things did not go quite so well this time, however. Taking off at 11.20 a.m., Lidsey and his pilot, Fred Gay, arrived on-station as planned, and made wireless contact with the battery. Jack watched as the Canadian guns fired seven heavy rounds towards the Germans, but none of them exploded. Giving the sortie up, they returned to Bruay and decided to drive to the battery to see what had gone wrong, only to be met by a furious battery commander who 'cursed them very nastily'. The guns had been firing shells with delayed-action fuses, dropping the rounds 200 yards beyond the intended target and expecting Jack to see the bursts some time after the shells had landed and then transmit corrections accordingly. Lidsey, however, did not know this, and had been looking much closer around the target, watching to see the rounds explode on impact. Of the Canadian gunner, Lidsey left a very terse comment in his diary saying that he 'shall NOT shoot with him again'.

Friday 26 January was bitterly cold. With a ground temperature of around twenty degrees Fahrenheit (almost minus seven Celsius), Jack and Lieutenant Morris took off at 10.00 a.m. for an artillery shoot but came back fifteen minutes later with a faulty engine. They went off again at 11.00 a.m., but found their battery already busy firing, so they decided to do a reconnaissance of enemy positions instead. They were carrying two 20lb bombs, and attacked a set of railway tracks but failed to hit the target. Instead they 'missed a house by about 20 yards, [the bombs] falling into a field'. By the time they landed, they had been in the air for almost two and a half hours, and 'returned nearly frozen stiff'.

For the next seven days, Jack went off on a Lewis Gun course at Camiers, a coastal town in the Pas-de-Calais next door to the British Expeditionary Force's training camp at Étaples. Accommodated in a sea-front hotel, he noted that it was probably a lovely place in the summer, but in January, with a forty miles per hour onshore wind and seventeen degrees Fahrenheit (about minus eight Centigrade), it was bitterly cold. There was only one fire in the hotel, around which the course members huddled trying to keep warm in the evenings. Lectures were given in a 'beastly hut', with temperatures still hovering around freezing, and with nothing new coming across in terms of learning – it was 'a lot of prattle about the Lewis Gun' that they had heard 'thousands of times before', the more so for Jack since he had already been on such a course while with the Oxfordshires back in August 1916. The monotony was broken only by firing a few rounds of ammunition on the range, but even this was something Jack was by now well versed in, having done it for real.

Although the course was boring, cold and tedious, being sent on it had saved Jack's life. On Thursday 1 February, he received word from Bruay that two No. 16 Squadron comrades had been shot down, their fate unknown, but 'fell in a spinning nose dive in Hunland ... probably both killed'. The unfortunate crew were Jack's pilot from the near-disastrous trip of 15 January, Percival Murray, and his observer, a 24-year-old Canadian lieutenant named Duncan McRae. McRae was only flying with Murray because Jack was away on the Lewis Gun course, otherwise Lidsey would have been in the front seat. Murray and McRae had taken off that afternoon on a photo reconnaissance task north of Arras; at around 3.10 p.m. a Canadian artillery unit reported seeing a fight between three RFC aircraft and four Germans, observing one British machine shot down behind enemy lines five minutes later.

Their loss marked a significant day for No. 16 Squadron, for the German pilot who had shot Murray and McRae down was none other than Manfred von Richthofen, the Red Baron, marking his first victory over No. 16 Squadron and his nineteenth to date. With his wingman, *Leutnant* Karl Allemröder, giving cover, von Richthofen had closed right in behind the BE2 and fired 150 rounds from only an aeroplane's length away – point-blank range – seeing it curve away to the right apparently out of control.[141] The stricken BE2 crashed into the barbed wire directly in front of the enemy trenches from where German troops extricated the crew, severely wounded, from the wreckage and took them prisoner, but both Murray and McRae died the following day. McRae, a banker from Ontario, had only applied for a transfer from the infantry to the

RFC in December 1916, so had been with No. 16 Squadron for just a couple of weeks; he had arrived in France with the Canadian Expeditionary Force the previous August and had already lost his brother, also killed in action. Murray, a native of Country Durham and aged just twenty, had abandoned his university studies (he was reading mechanical engineering at Durham) on the outbreak of war and immediately volunteered for service with the Durham Light Infantry. He had qualified as a pilot in October 1916.[142]

The Red Baron had taken command of *Jasta 11* just one month earlier. Initially, von Richthofen had not wanted to lead his own squadron: 'I must say I was annoyed. I had learnt to work so well with my comrades of Boelcke's[143] Squadron and now I had to begin all over again working hand in hand with different people. It was a beastly nuisance.'[144] But the skies over Vimy and Arras were to prove fruitful hunting grounds for him, and it was not long before he changed his tune: 'I had never imagined that it would be so delightful to command a chasing squadron. Even in my dreams I had not imagined that there would ever be a Richthofen's squadron of aeroplanes.'[145] His *Jasta* was equipped with the Albatros D.III, a new fighter that had only entered service the previous December. The aeroplane had suffered some teething problems, notably rib and leading-edge failures of the lower wing – von Richthofen himself was to experience one such episode on 24 January 1917, prompting a grounding order for the Albatros until new wings could be hurried to the front-line *Jastas*. In the meantime, von Richthofen flew a Halberstadt, an older design and not as capable, but it was all that was available. He was flying a Halberstadt on the day he downed Murray and McCrae, but modifications to the Albatros wings were completed swiftly and the grounding order was lifted on 19 February, when von Richthofen most likely went straight back to flying the D.III, the better machine. No. 16 Squadron's CO Paul Maltby wrote that, such was the threat posed by the German Albatros to his BE2s, that observers often had to abandon their primary role and simply act as lookouts against a surprise attack.[146]

The Lewis Gun course finished the next day, Jack having found it a complete waste of time. His exasperation was to be compounded by a slow, tortuous journey back to Bruay in the freezing weather. He arrived at Étaples only to find that his movement order, without which he could not travel, was nowhere to be found. Four hours of searching for it in every Army transport depot in town finally turned it up, back in the office that he had first enquired in, only then to discover that there were no more troop train movements scheduled for that day. Next morning, Lidsey got up at 5.00 a.m., having secured the only available bed in a YMCA the previous night (he was supposed to have slept in a rest camp under canvas, but given the cold, he was 'not having any'), to catch a train at 6.30 a.m., which then did not leave until 9.30 a.m. The trip was to prove as bad as that of the previous day: 'When the train did start, she crawled all the way, stopping here, there and everywhere. Arrived at Béthune at 9pm – twelve hours going 60 miles. Phoned the Squadron for a car to take me back to Bruay.'

Finally arriving at the aerodrome on 4 February, he discovered that there was both good and bad news waiting for him. The good news was that he had been recommended and approved as 'flying officer observer' and was therefore now entitled to wear the observer's badge on the left breast of his uniform. His probation was over; he was now a fully-fledged member of the Royal Flying Corps aircrew fraternity. The bad news was that No. 16 Squadron had lost three more men that day. Second Lieutenant Noel Vernham, a 27-year-old married man from London, Lieutenant Alfred Steele, another Londoner aged twenty-five, and Lieutenant James Boyd (a Canadian, also twenty-seven) had all been killed. Steele and Boyd had courageously forced down an enemy aircraft from *Jasta 2* but were almost immediately shot down themselves by *Leutnant* Erich König of the same *Jasta*, his fourth victory. Vernham's pilot, Lieutenant Herbert Massey, had fought to keep their blazing BE2 from smashing into the ground and managed, with immense courage and skill, to crash-land the machine. Despite side-slipping all the way down in an effort to keep the flames away from himself and Vernham, Massey had been badly burned, but at least he had survived, unlike his observer. They had been shot down by another of Germany's fighter aces, Werner Voss, becoming his fifth victim. Unlike the privileged von Richthofen, the 20-year-old Voss came from an ordinary family. Volunteering for the army on the outbreak of war, he joined the cavalry and then transferred to the German Air Service, where he proved to be a natural pilot. Voss was a great friend and rival of von Richthofen, having flown together earlier in the war;

indeed, the Red Baron thought of Voss as the only pilot capable of challenging him as the 'ace of aces'.

The ferocious combats in the skies above No. 16 Squadron's patch continued. The next day, Lieutenant Arthur Burlton, with 'his leave warrant in his pocket' was attacked by three enemy aircraft, leaving a hole 'six inches in diameter in his tail plane and put six bullets through the undercarriage'. The extremely fortunate Burlton got home without a scratch, and with his precious leave warrant intact. The date of 6 February saw another lucky escape when Captain Davison force-landed his badly damaged BE2 after being set upon by German fighters. He counted eighteen holes through the fuselage, with three bullets discovered lodged in his seat cushion.

Lidsey next flew on Wednesday 7 February on a photo reconnaissance mission. He had managed to expose five images when the BE's engine began to misfire, causing his pilot, Lieutenant Morris, to force-land the aircraft near Houdain. The sick motor proved to be a life-saver, though, as they were being lined up as a target by a German Albatros fighter[147] when they had to abandon their task. Once again, two FE8s of No. 40 Squadron came to the rescue, attacking the German machine. Jack saw the enemy firing 'bullets at them that had a shrapnel effect, thirty or forty little puffs of white smoke all around our machines'. On the ground, he lost sight of the fight going on above, and 'did not see the end of the scrap', but the two FE8s, piloted by Sergeant W. Walder and Lieutenant W. Cox, saw 'the hostile aircraft heading for Douai losing height – circled and was seen to land E[ast] of Henin Lietard'.[148] With their engine now repaired (a mechanical pump had worked loose), Jack and Morris took off once again and made their way back to Bruay – Major Maltby wrote 'Good' underneath Lidsey's log book entry for the sortie, no doubt pleased that they had brought the BE2, and themselves, home in one piece. In the squadron office, Jack found the best news of all waiting for him – a warrant for two weeks' leave with his name on it, and he was to go that very night; it was his first period of leave since arriving in France almost two years previously. He caught the midnight train from Bruay to Boulogne, arriving at 8.00 a.m. just in time for a hurried breakfast before the boat for England sailed at 10.30 a.m. By 3.00 p.m. that afternoon he was in London, where he made his way to Paddington for the train home to Banbury.

There are no clues as to how Jack spent his leave, since he made no diary entries for the whole time that he was at home. His last day of furlough was supposed to be Wednesday 21 February, but on returning home from the theatre that night he went to order a taxi to take him to the station, only to be told that there were no leave trains scheduled for the next day, so he gained an extra twenty-four hours – 'what rejoicing, one more day of bliss'. The following day was difficult, having to say his goodbyes once more to the family before he headed off back to France. Catching the boat train early on Friday morning from London's Victoria station, Lidsey sailed from Folkestone at 10.00 a.m., a journey slowed by fog in the English Channel. At Boulogne, he caught the 3.00 p.m. train, arriving in Béthune at midnight. After a long day's travel, all Jack then wanted to do was sleep, but when he arrived at his billet at around 1.00 a.m on Saturday morning, he found the door locked and his landlady away. With no other options open to him, he headed to Bruay and the officers' mess at the aerodrome, where he settled down for the night on some chairs in the ante-room.

Waking up stiff and cold a few hours later, Jack was at least pleased to discover that the weather was bad and that there was no prospect of flying. However, during his absence, the squadron had moved into 'wretchedly cold and soakingly damp huts' out on the airfield, having been turned out of their comfortable billets in Bruay. Lidsey decided to stay on at his billet, paying for it from his own pocket, but knowing that sooner or later it would be noticed that he was not with everyone else and that he would have to move out. Still, in the short term, it was worth it for the extra comfort.

The accommodation problems were not the only bad news – there were faces missing from the squadron too. Second Lieutenant Leslie Munn had taken 20-year-old Second Lieutenant Ernest Lindley, a new pilot, aloft for a familiarisation trip over the front line on 16 February and they had failed to return. There was an outside chance that they had got lost, landed on the wrong side of the lines and had been taken prisoner, but word came through later that both had been killed. They had been shot down by Karl Allemröder, von Richthofen's wingman from the attack on Murray and McRae on 1 February. Munn was killed instantly, while Lindley died later from his wounds. They were Allemröder's first victims, and, given Lindley's lack of experience, probably made for easy pickings.

No. 16 Squadron had apparently, however, managed to gain some measure of revenge for their recent losses while Jack had been away. On 8 February, Lieutenant Fred Gay had been airborne with Corporal Paxman in the front seat on a photography task when they were attacked by an enemy fighter. Paxman gave the German forty rounds from his Lewis Gun and saw several tracers enter the hostile machine before the Lewis Gun jammed due to oil congealing,[149] but it seemed that the damage had already been done – the 'Hun' went down, 'diving vertically towards the ground',[150] although it soon disappeared from their view. According to Lidsey, the hostile aircraft 'went down completely crashed near Farbus; great rejoicings'. Gay and Paxman's machine had eight bullet holes in it, with two bracing wires shot away. But it seems that the celebrations were undeserved, for there are no records of a German aircraft being shot down anywhere near Farbus that day, and no official 'kill' claim was made by a BE2 – even the British airmen's own combat report confirms that neither of them saw their quarry hit the ground because they had lost sight of it.

Lidsey next flew on 25 February, the first time since he had gone away on leave on the 7th. He probably wanted to ease himself gently back into the routine, but no such luck. He was paired with Second Lieutenant Taylor, a newly arrived, newly- qualified pilot who had never flown with a passenger before and had not yet seen the enemy lines. Jack was distinctly unimpressed, and, probably with the fates of Munn and the novice Lindley a few days earlier still fresh in his mind, described the experience as 'not a pleasant job'. Still, they were only up for half an hour as thick fog closed in, making artillery observation impossible.

Good news came through later that day from one of the other squadrons in the area; a BE2 from No. 2 Squadron,[151] based at Hesdigneul just a few miles from Bruay, had managed to bring down, in flames, an enemy machine that had attacked it. Lidsey told his diary, perhaps with some irony, that 'they will soon learn better manners than to attack a poor, harmless-looking BE2c'.

The next day, Lidsey flew three times, and each time turned back due

to either poor weather or mechanical problems. But his travails were
nothing compared to those of two of his No. 16 Squadron comrades,
Second Lieutenant Robert Jack and his pilot, Lieutenant Harry Bagot.
The pair were flying close to Vimy Ridge when they were attacked by
Werner Voss. Bagot somehow managed to bring the BE2 down under
control despite being badly wounded and with severe damage to the
aircraft (Lidsey remarked that 'most of his controls were shot away'), but
the machine crashed upon landing. Bagot had taken one of Voss's
bullets through his upper lip, and another in his 'sit-upon', as Lidsey
delicately put it, and then broke his wrist in the subsequent crash-land-
ing, when he was thrown some fifteen yards from the wreckage. Robert
Jack was in a worse state, however, having been shot in the head; he
died at around 2.00 a.m. the next morning in a British field hospital.
Lidsey says in his diary that 'a de Havilland pilot brought down the
Hun who brought Bagot down. The de Havilland pilot[152] was shot in
the leg by an explosive bullet and was taken to the same hospital as Bagot
at Aubigny.' There is obviously some confusion in Lidsey's account as
Voss was not shot down that day; indeed, Bagot and Robert Jack were
only his ninth victim out of a total of forty-eight. Werner Voss was
eventually shot down and killed on 23 September 1917 during a furious
dogfight with RFC fighters, one of which was piloted by the British ace
James McCudden, VC; Voss fought seven British aircraft alone that day
before being brought down. McCudden later said: 'As long as I live I shall
never forget my admiration for that German pilot, who single-handed
fought seven of us for ten minutes and also put some bullets through
all our machines. His flying was wonderful, his courage magnificent, and
in my opinion, he was the bravest German airman whom it has been
my privilege to see fight.'

On the morning that Robert Jack died, 27 February, Lidsey and
Lieutenant Morris took off early, at 7.00 a.m. and in very bad visibility.
The cloud base was down to 1,000 feet, forcing them even lower so as to
keep the ground in sight. As they crossed over the front line, they were met
with 'volumes' of machine-gun fire from the German trenches, and they
also saw several enemy aircraft away in the distance. Deciding that
discretion was the better part of valour, Morris turned the BE2 around
and headed back to Bruay, and they were back on the ground by 9.30 a.m.

With dud weather the next day, the last day of February 1917, the squadron attended Robert Jack's funeral at nearby Aubigny cemetery, with Lidsey acting as one of the four pall bearers. He described it as a 'very sad proceeding' but noted that the padre was 'exceedingly nice'.

Chapter Eleven

No. 16 Squadron, Royal Flying Corps, 1 – 20 March 1917

As March 1917 arrived, so did a step change in the level of activity in the Arras area. The new commander of the French Army, General Robert Nivelle, had formulated an ambitious plan to bring about a sudden, decisive victory against the Germans. Nivelle's idea was for a huge and overwhelming attack, supported by the mass use of artillery, which would end the war within forty-eight hours, and with only 10,000 casualties. The plan called for a major assault by the French in the Aisne region, to be preceded by a British diversionary offensive some fifty miles to the north in the Arras sector designed to draw the Germans' attention away from the main French thrust. Political support for Nivelle had initially been firm – he was after all the hero of Verdun, where his tactic of using a 'creeping barrage'[153] had proved spectacularly successful against the German defenders, and he insisted that it could be repeated, this time bringing about a complete German collapse on the Western Front. Nivelle's self-assuredness and reputation added to the notion that the plan was foolproof.

However, like at Verdun before the Allied Somme offensive the previous year, the Germans had plans of their own. In an effort to make the Western Front easier to defend, they pulled back from part of Nivelle's intended attack sector to their strong and well-prepared defensive position known as the Hindenburg Line. This shrewd strategic withdrawal straightened the front line in favour of the Germans, first by removing two salients, one around Bapaume, and the other further south at Noyon, and secondly by reducing the length of the front line, thereby freeing up around fourteen divisions to contribute towards the defence of the Hindenburg Line. As they withdrew, the Germans carried out a 'scorched earth' policy, destroying everything – towns, roads, crops and water supplies – in their wake. Sensing an opportunity, the French General Louis d'Espèrey appealed to Nivelle to launch a major attack to rout the Germans while they were retreating and before they had time to bed themselves down in the Hindenburg Line, but Nivelle conceded only to a limited assault to capture the old German front line – an opportunity was lost. Doubts began to be cast over Nivelle's grand plan, both politically and militarily, but Nivelle was adamant that he knew what he was doing, and that the plan would work. The French attack was scheduled for mid-April, with the British feint going in the week before.

The British sector of Arras was dominated by Vimy Ridge, a narrow escarpment to the north of Arras just over four miles long and rising to almost 500 feet above sea level at its highest point, and which commanded the landscape for miles around. The Germans had been on top of the ridge since 1914; twice in 1915 the French had tried to dislodge them but to no avail, taking well over 100,000 casualties for their trouble. Now, in 1917, it was the troops of the Canadian Corps, four divisions of infantry, who faced Vimy Ridge, and it would fall to them to take the heights as part of the British contribution to Nivelle's grand strategy. The British high command was determined not to repeat the harsh experiences of the Somme the year before and resolved to put into action its hard-learned lessons. This time, meticulous planning; thorough practice and training using full-size replicas of the German trenches; carefully timed attacks; and effective coordination of artillery with the infantry, would win the day, along with the extensive use of tunnels to bring troops to the front line to hide their movement from the enemy. Nothing was to be left to chance.

So important was the artillery to the British part of the plan that it was deployed in far greater numbers than at the Battle of the Somme the previous year. The increase was considerable, particularly with regard to the heavy howitzer guns – three times more of these monster weapons were positioned than in 1916, and a larger allocation of shells meant that the rate of artillery fire would be far higher too. Improved shells and fuses would this time ensure that maximum damage would be done to the enemy barbed-wire defences, destroying them just before the advancing Canadians arrived at the German trenches. An intricate fire support plan was devised by Brigadier General Edward Morrison, the gunners' commander, and crucial to the success of the artillery would be the role of air power, as, without aerial reconnaissance and spotting, the guns would be firing blind. Not only that, but air superiority over the German Air Service would be vital to keep the enemy's prying eyes away from the British build-up to preserve the element of surprise. To that end, the Royal Flying Corps deployed some twenty-five squadrons along the Arras front, with No. 16 Squadron being allocated exclusively to the Canadian Corps. To help cope with the surge in work, No. 16 Squadron was sent an extra two flights of four aircraft each from both Nos 5 and 10 Squadrons, bringing the squadron strength up to thirty-two aeroplanes, a quantity that Paul Maltby found to be 'too large a unit to command effectively', and I and my staff found ourselves thoroughly over-worked'.[154] With the date of the British attack set for Easter Monday, 9 April 1917, Jack Lidsey and his fellow observers were to be the eyes of the guns.

No. 16 Squadron went straight into the assault preparations on 1 March. Jack was roused at 3.00 a.m. with orders to take off with Lieutenant Morris on a 'special mission in connection with a trench raid'. Leaving the ground at 6.40 a.m., they had lost sight of the ground by the time they had reached just 400 feet due to low cloud, and were back on the ground after only ten minutes. Lidsey took off again at 2.20 p.m., after morning mist had dispersed, with Lieutenant George Underwood as his pilot, carrying out a successful artillery registration task with No. 3 Canadian Siege Battery. Noting that the sky 'was thick with Huns', Jack and Underwood nevertheless got home safely, and later went to dinner with the Canadian gunners, doubtless part of the close liaison between No. 16 Squadron and the artillery that would be so important to the success of the coming 'boost'.

A couple of days of poor weather followed, allowing the aircrew to let off some steam through sport. Jack played rugby for the first time in his life, enjoying it immensely, although he felt the pleasure would be greater with more experience. He was continually penalised 'for doing things I did not know were wrong'.

Sunday 4 March was to prove very nearly Jack's last day of existence. If he had nine lives, he was to use up two of them that day. A strong wind was blowing, making flying tricky, but the work with the artillery had to be done. Lidsey was paired with Morris, with whom he had flown when Morris was a novice back in January. This time they 'had a most awful take-off in a strong wind, very nearly crashed. This sent him [Morris] practically off his head, so that he nearly lost control of the machine. Had three tries to get back to the aerodrome before landing. On landing he fell forward over the controls practically in a faint. During the flight, which lasted 30 minutes, he stalled the machine three times and side-slipped twice; I do not want another such experience, it was decidedly unpleasant.'

Relieved to back on terra firma, Jack was informed that he was to fly again, this time with the more experienced Captain Neale, his flight commander, as his pilot. They took off at 2.30 in the afternoon to take photographs over the German side of the lines but returned just ten minutes later due to engine trouble. Swapping to another BE2 (the same machine in which Lidsey had had the experience with Morris earlier) they left the ground again at 3.20 p.m.; an hour later they were at 5,000 feet over Bailleul, about three miles inside enemy territory, when they 'were attacked by two Huns, one being the man with a machine painted red who has done us so much damage. I opened fire with my gun first and they cleared off. During the two hours that we were up we saw nine other Huns but did not fight any of them. Exposed four plates all of which were underexposed.'

Back at Bruay, Neale and Lidsey compiled their combat report:[155] 'We were attacked by two enemy machines just N[orth] of Bailleul. At the time we were flying due E[ast]. Capt Neale turned the machine so as to bring the rear gun [the Strange Mount] into action. The red machine then dived on our tail, the observer fired about 10 rounds & the enemy then cleared away without firing.'[156] Jack Lidsey had survived his first encounter with Manfred von Richthofen, the Red Baron. Others were not so lucky that day – von Richthofen shot down a No. 2 Squadron BE2 and a Sopwith 1½ Strutter from No. 43 Squadron, his twenty-second and twenty-third victims. Major Maltby was evidently impressed with Lidsey and Neale's deeds as he wrote of them in a notebook he kept entitled the 'Honours

Book',[157] perhaps with the intention of recommending them for a bravery award, although nothing came of it.

Tuesday 6 March was to prove a black day in No. 16 Squadron's short history. Jack notes 'great aerial activity, did not fly myself, had day's rest … numerous Huns were brought down by fighting squadrons during the day'. He was fortunate not to be in the air – the daily RFC communiqué records that: 'Hostile aircraft were exceptionally active during the day and a great number of combats took place. About 70 hostile aeroplanes were observed opposite the First Army front; 23 of these crossed the lines. Much aerial fighting took place all along the Front throughout the day, during which three hostile machines were brought down and at least three others driven down damaged. Four of our machines were brought down, and seven others are missing.'[158]

No. 16 Squadron's first casualties that day were George Underwood and his observer, Second Lieutenant Albert Watts, who were carrying out a photo-reconnaissance sortie when they were brought down by a German fighter over Givenchy during the late morning. In his diary, Jack says that they came down 'under control, but in the Hun lines', but in fact both Underwood and Watts had been killed (their bodies were never found), shot down by one of von Richthofen's *Jasta 11*. *Leutnant* Kurt Wolff had claimed his first victory, but it was almost his last; seeing Underwood's machine fall to earth, fellow No. 16 Squadron pilot Arthur Burlton swung in to attack Wolff, a brave move against a German Albatros with a BE2. As he came in from one side and slightly above, Burlton and his observer, Second Lieutenant F.H. Baguley, opened fire with their two Lewis Guns. Burlton gave Wolff a full drum from his weapon and saw the enemy aircraft appear to go down out of control, but he lost sight of his adversary as he had his hands full flying the BE2 and changing the magazine on his Lewis Gun. Baguley thought he saw the hostile aeroplane crash, but, flying low over the area, they saw no further trace of the German aircraft,[159] even though Lidsey told his diary that it 'absolutely crashed in the Bois de la Folie'. Wolff had in fact survived unscathed, going on to claim thirty-three victories before being killed the following September. Von Richthofen described him as 'a delicate-looking little fellow in whom nobody could have suspected a redoubtable hero'.[160]

Manfred von Richthofen himself had not had the best of mornings.

Engaged in a dogfight with British FE8 fighters of No. 40 Squadron, the Red Baron had had his engine and fuel tanks damaged (most probably from rounds fired by Lieutenant Edwin Benbow, who had helped save Lidsey's life on 4 December 1916) and had made a forced landing on the German side of the lines. Undeterred, he returned that afternoon to his aerodrome at La Brayelle (after being royally entertained to a champagne and oyster lunch by the engineer officer who had recovered him after he landed), clambered into another machine, and took off again. This time he happened upon a pair of No. 16 Squadron BE2s, the first of which was piloted by Second Lieutenant Gerald Gosset-Bibby, flying with Lieutenant Geoffrey Brichta as his observer, operating close to Souchez (over the British side of the front) on an artillery observation sortie. With Allemröder once again acting as his wingman, von Richthofen 'attacked two enemy artillery flyers at a low altitude over the other side [of the lines]. The wings of the plane I attacked came off; it dashed down and smashed on the ground.'[161] Lidsey recorded that 'Lt Bibby [sic] with Lt Brichta (machine gun officer) were brought down in flames 500 yds on our side of the lines, both killed'.

Twenty-year-old Gosset-Bibby was new to No. 16 Squadron (he had been with them only a matter of days), having qualified as a pilot just the previous month, although he had formerly been an NCO observer and had seen aerial service during the Battle of the Somme the preceding summer.[162] His father, a retired clergyman and former headmaster of Kimbolton School in Cambridgeshire, wrote to Major Maltby from Bedford on 13 March to say that 'it was such a great relief to his mother and sister to know that he had passed away without much suffering[163] & that his poor body was resting quietly in the British cemetery in Barlin in French soil. We grieve too for his observer Lt Brichta.'[164] In the same letter, the Reverend Gosset-Bibby said that 'you [Maltby] mention that the German machines were swifter than that Gerald had – it may interest you to know that an engineer (billeted with us) has for some time been engaged on a more powerful Le Rhône aeroplane engine & that it may assist our pilots before long'. For Paul Maltby and his long-suffering squadron, better engines and aircraft could not arrive soon enough.

The musically gifted Geoffrey Brichta had been born in Austria in 1884 to British parents (his father was a doctor who practised in Vienna) before returning to England. As a young man, he emigrated to Canada in 1908 where he ran the North Battleford Piano Company and was a member of the local militia, the Saskatchewan Light Horse. Brichta arrived in France in March 1916 with the Canadian cavalry before becoming an RFC observer in late September that year. He was married with three children and was thirty-two years old.[165]

Their deaths were almost certainly contributed to by the new pilot's lack of experience, and may well have been avoidable. Gosset-Bibby had apparently tried to shake von Richthofen off by diving away from him, but had he heeded the advice of his flight commander, Captain Eric Routh, who had warned him previously about not employing that particular tactic in a BE2, he and Brichta might have survived:[166] 'I especially told Bibby [sic] to master sharp turns but he would never do it, and I equally told him never to dive straight away from a Hun, which he was seen to do. He would have been perfectly alright if he had kept his head. I am very sorry for both of them; Brichta was a married man and I liked him very much. He was a very stout fellow.'[167]

With his first target duly despatched, Manfred von Richthofen then turned his attention to the second BE2 he had spotted, which was being flown by Flight Sergeant Sidney Quicke with Captain L.E. Claremont as his observer in the front seat. They saw Gosset-Bibby and Brichta going down 'in a spinning nose-dive'[168] (presumably it was they who also reported Gosset-Bibby trying to dive away) and Sid hurriedly turned his machine westwards to get away. Almost immediately, Claremont heard machine-gun fire and Quicke saw a white-painted enemy fighter (probably Allemröder) ahead of him shortly before a red German aircraft appeared on their tail – von Richthofen had been above them, obscured from their view by the BE2's upper wing centre-section. Claremont stood up, heaved his Lewis Gun on to the Strange Mount between the two cockpits, and opened fire rearwards over Quicke's head with a sustained burst of seventy rounds. Von Richthofen plainly felt that this BE2 was not worth the trouble (or perhaps his aircraft had taken hits), since Claremont saw him 'turn away sharply and fly back over the enemy lines'.[169] The British aeroplane had not escaped unscathed, however; von Richthofen had scored hits on the BE2's upper left aileron, which was completely inoperable, and shattered an outer strut (Lidsey described the machine as 'shot about badly'). Nursing his wounded aircraft back over friendly lines, Sid Quicke skilfully side-slipped it to a forced, but safe, landing in a field near Camblain-l'Abbé.

No. 16 Squadron's bad day was not quite over yet, though. Lieutenant Osbert Knight, flying with Second Air Mechanic E.D. Harvey as his observer, was to return safely to Bruay having been attacked by German fighters and wounded in the arm by a bullet. After a day of frantic activity, No. 16 Squadron was down by three aircraft, with four men dead and one wounded.

Geoffrey Brichta had been the squadron's machine-gun officer, and his death meant that Lidsey now assumed that mantle, probably in view of his recent attendance on the Lewis Gun course. The role carried a great deal of responsibility, given that the Lewis Gun was the BE2's only means of self-defence, and it would not have been bestowed on him lightly by Major Maltby. Jack was expected to have a thorough knowledge and understanding of the weapon and be able to give instruction and training on it, including stripping, cleaning and firing the gun; the causes and clearance of stoppages; the principles of aiming; and filling and changing the magazine. He was required to keep a log of every occasion when the Lewis Gun was fired in anger, and to report back to both the squadron and higher headquarters with comments and suggestions on how to use it more effectively. In addition to the weapons carried by the squadron's aircraft, he was also to oversee the siting and maintenance of Bruay's ground-based anti-aircraft machine guns. Most importantly, he was responsible for examining his fellow observers' and pilots' competence with the weapon.[170] A memorandum from the commanding general, 1st Brigade RFC to No. 1 Wing RFC stressed the importance of the subject: 'Please impress on Squadron Commanders the urgency of making every observer thoroughly efficient in the handling of the Lewis Gun, and shooting from the air. Continuous practice is necessary to become expert. If observers have perfect confidence in their own shooting it will be found that a better defense [sic] will be made against attacks from hostile aircraft, and that casualties will be less frequent. Perhaps all observers in your Wing are not aware that two Albatros scouts have recently been brought down by BE observers.'[171]

Major Maltby agreed, as he felt that new pilots were being sent out from training to the front-line squadrons with thoroughly inadequate experience on the Lewis Gun, stating that 'a great mistake was to send them out knowing so little about air gunnery … many hardly knew how their guns worked, much less how to use them or how to manoeuvre if attacked. Hence the numerous casualties amongst the last joined.'[172]

Firing the weapon on a range against a static target was all well and good, but to further sharpen the aircrews' skill with the Lewis Gun, squadrons were ordered to indent for clay-pigeon shooting equipment. Great faith was placed by the RFC in the sport as a way of learning the art of deflection shooting – aiming the gun ahead of the target so that the enemy aircraft would fly into the bullet stream, instead of the rounds passing harmlessly behind. Bemused squadron armourers soon found themselves the custodians of traps, clays and shotguns for use out on the airfield by the pilots and observers.

Snow and strong winds returned to Bruay for the next few days. Betraying his delight at not having to risk his life in the air, Jack called the weather 'beautifully dud'. He spent the time examining his comrades on the intricacies of the Lewis Gun in his new-found role but, obviously unimpressed with their performance, he 'did not pass any'. He also visited various Canadian infantry units to arrange practice contact patrols for the coming attack and found them to be 'an awfully nice lot of fellows'.

As soon as the weather cleared, the squadron went back to its vital work in support of the Canadian Corps. The morning of Sunday 11 March saw Jack Lidsey working with 2nd Canadian Siege Battery, tasked to register the fall of their shot against a German defensive position. Unable to find the target, however, Lidsey and his pilot, Lieutenant Taylor, spent their time doing a visual reconnaissance of the German lines to glean whatever information they could about the enemy. Spotting three German artillery batteries, numerous trenches, tracks, barbed-wire defences and supply dumps, Jack carefully noted down everything he saw and marked their positions on his map – anything might be useful in the coming days. The Germans knew what the British aircraft was up to, though, and gave it a 'warm reception with machine-gun fire from the trenches, putting two bullets through our tail plane when flying at 4,000 feet'.

That afternoon, Lidsey was once again to dice with death due to the shortcomings of the BE2: 'Left the ground again, or rather crawled off it with Lt Stewart, on practice contact patrol. The machine would not leave the ground; we ran across the aerodrome, then across a ploughed field at 60 mph, expecting to be turned upside-down at any minute. Then we saw just in front of us a mangold heap, two ricks and some telegraph wires. Stewart yanked the stick back and the old bus just crawled over. Great cheers from me, I thought we were in for a good old crash.'

No doubt grateful to be back on the ground, Jack spent the rest of the day lecturing the infantry on contact patrols and visiting various units in the front line to arrange future practices in the same. It was a busy time, with no prospect of respite on the horizon.

Next day, Lidsey flew for the first time with Flight Sergeant Quicke as his pilot. Sidney Herbert Quicke was a 28-year-old Londoner who had lived at home with his widowed mother in East Finchley before he joined the RFC in 1913, just a year after its formation and one before the outbreak of the First World War. He was one of the first to go to France when war came in August 1914, as a mechanic with No. 4 Squadron who were then operating a French aeroplane, the Farman MF11 Shorthorn. Sid loved aircraft and flying, and before long made it his aim to become aircrew. By March 1916 he was an observer but, still not satisfied, Quicke qualified as a sergeant pilot on 27 November in the same year, having gained his Royal Aero Club Aviator's Certificate (number 3890), and was posted to No. 16 Squadron.

Taking off at 10.00 a.m., the pair carried out a practice contact patrol with the 8th Canadian Infantry Brigade, part of the 3rd Canadian Division who would assault Vimy Ridge the following month. This was not to be a routine practice, though, since it was to be performed in front of Prince Arthur of Connaught, aide-de-camp to Field Marshal Haig and grandson of Queen Victoria. The sortie was a complete failure, as 'everything that the signallers could do wrong, they did'. Evidently, much more practice with the ground forces was going to be needed if the coming offensive was to be anything near a success, and Jack pronounced himself 'fed up'. That afternoon was spent principally with the officers and senior NCOs of Princess Patricia's Canadian Light Infantry of the Canadian 7th Infantry Brigade, 3rd Canadian Division, again lecturing on, and organising, contact patrols, before doing more of the same later, this time with the 42nd Battalion (Royal Highlanders of Canada). Finishing the liaison work in the early evening, Lidsey then paid a visit to the 8th Canadian Brigade, with whose signallers he had had so much trouble that morning, where he 'cursed the Brigadier and his signalling officer'. The brigadier 'humbly apologised' and invited Lidsey to stay for dinner. For such a junior officer to roundly curse a brigadier general to his face, and to elicit a meek apology, is highly unusual – if it was indeed true. Still, the visit seems to have paid dividends, since Jack and Quicke repeated the exercise with the brigade three days later on 15 March, reporting the sortie this time as 'a fairly successful show'.

Every day brought more and more training with the Canadian troops. If the weather was good, No. 16 Squadron spent its time doing practice contact patrols and artillery shoots. If it was bad, then lectures were the order of the day, either to the signallers to ensure effective communications, or to the infantry to theorise cooperation between aircraft and ground forces. With less than a month to go until the British went into the attack in the Arras sector, the pace of work was relentless. Jack wrote to his mother at Hardwick House on 14 March, telling her:

I am working like a Trojan now, the officer who generally does all the infantry co-operation has gone on leave, so I have all his work to do as well as my machine gun job. I have been lecturing on infantry co-operation nearly all day for the last four days; today I had 90 signallers, tomorrow I have the same number coming here. The weather has been very dud indeed lately, raining practically the whole time, the roads are swimming in mud. Anyone that walks about gets plastered from head to foot by the splashes from the motor lorries.

Lidsey and Quicke flew together again on 16 March, this time on a practice contact patrol with the 6th Canadian Infantry Brigade. The sortie was a success, which Jack followed up with a visit to the brigade's headquarters at nearby Maisnil-Bouche that evening, to discuss the day's results. An evidently pleased commanding brigadier general invited him to stay for dinner, with Lidsey describing him as a 'very nice man'.

Saturday 17 March 1917 saw Jack and Sid paired once more. By now, they were beginning to establish a partnership in the air, developing the trust between them that comes from experience and familiarity. They took off at 10.30 that morning and did a 'very successful' practice contact patrol, this time with the 44th Canadian Infantry Battalion, a unit raised in Manitoba and proudly bearing that region's name. The weather was starting to close in, however, with the wind picking up to gale force later in the day and playing havoc at Bruay, where two BEs were picked up by the wind and smashed to pieces, thankfully whilse parked and with no crews in them. Fortunately, Lidsey and Quicke were back on the ground before the worst of the storm set in, but Second Lieutenant Charles Crow, flying with Quicke's old observer Claremont, was not quite so lucky. Coming back later in the day and struggling to keep the BE2 steady in the wind, Crow's engine suddenly cut out when the machine was just 200 feet from the ground, almost back to safety. Crashing into a hay rick short of the aerodrome, Claremont suffered a blow to the head, which gave him a severe laceration and concussion, just enough to guarantee him a 'Blighty' wound and evacuation home. Crow escaped unscathed.

Claremont was not to be No. 16 Squadron's only casualty that day, though. Jack noted in his diary that 'Lieutenant Watt with Sergeant Howlett brought down just in our lines by the red Hun. Both killed.' George Watt and Ernest Howlett had taken off at 3.25 p.m. on an artillery observation sortie with the Canadian guns that were barraging German positions at Farbus on the southern edge of Vimy Ridge. Von Richthofen spotted them and tried several times to bring them down from the usual attacking position of above and behind, but with no success because the British machine was well protected from above by escorting fighters and could not be tempted into combat. If he was to add to his score with this BE2, von Richthofen realised he would have to try different tactics. Watt was keeping his aircraft at around 3,000 feet, so the Red Baron decided to try from below. Dropping down to a little over 2,000 feet, he came up from beneath his hapless adversary and opened fire with devastating effect: both the BE's wings folded, and the machine crashed to the ground between the lines with its crew dead.[173] This victory marked von Richthofen's second of the day; he had already shot down an FE2b belonging to No. 25 Squadron that morning.

George Watt had gone straight into the Royal Flying Corps as a pilot without any previous military service. A proud Scotsman and a fine rugby player, he was twenty-seven years old and had been with No. 16 Squadron for exactly two months.[174] He had earlier confided to his family his fears about the performance of the BE2, which had now tragically proved well founded. Writing to Major Maltby from Edinburgh on 22 March, Watt's father, also called George, said: 'I had a letter from him on the 16th of March saying that unless the Government gave them new machines, the whole Squadron would be wiped out. It is most distressing to think that our flying men with such machines have no chance with the Germans, and as my son said are thus "really at their mercy".[175]

Twenty-six-year-old Ernest Howlett was a Londoner from New Cross and had served with the East Kent Regiment in the trenches before volunteering for the RFC as an observer.[176] The two airmen's bodies were recovered from the wreckage and buried side by side in Bruay cemetery, close to No. 16 Squadron's home airfield. Despite their loss, life carried on – that evening, there were the preliminary bouts of the squadron boxing championships, which Lidsey recorded as a 'very good show'.

The weather prevented No. 16 Squadron from flying for the next few days. The only aerial activity was on 18 March when a Sopwith 1½ Strutter belonging to No. 43 Squadron crashed on the airfield at Bruay when its pilot came in too low while attempting to find out where he was.

As the preparations for the British offensive reached their peak, the German withdrawal to the Hindenburg Line was reaching its conclusion. Jack reported the retreat in his diary, noting the fall of Bapaume and Péronne to British troops, and that the French had advanced twelve miles in, along a front of forty-three miles. Word of the 'scorched earth' tactic had also reached British ears, and Lidsey recorded that the 'Huns were still retiring, burning villages as they go'. With foul weather still blowing on 20 March, on the pretext of buying a piano for the squadron mess, Jack managed to get a lift to St Omer, the RFC's headquarters airfield. There, he saw 'some of our new fighting machines; fine things'.[177] With the arrival of new aeroplanes, the Germans apparently on the run, and a 'boost' in the offing, perhaps things were beginning to look up for the Allies.

Chapter Twelve

No. 16 Squadron, Royal Flying Corps, Wednesday 21 March 1917

Wednesday 21 March 1917 dawned blustery, grey and wet, much the same as it had for the previous several days. Low cloud, borne on an icy wind blowing in from the east, scudded across the skies above the airfield at Bruay-la-Buissière, bringing heavy rain to the weary aircrew of No. 16 Squadron, Royal Flying Corps. Prospects for flying that day looked slim, but with the Arras offensive then only a fortnight or so away, every and any opportunity to gather intelligence against the enemy, or to register targets for the guns, would have needed to have been taken.

Some twenty-four miles to the south-east of Bruay, on the other side of the lines at La Brayelle airfield, near Douai, conditions would have been the same for Manfred von Richthofen's *Jasta 11*. The Red Baron had not claimed a kill for four days since shooting down Watt and Howlett on 17 March, and he would have been eager to add to his tally.

By mid-afternoon the weather had cleared sufficiently for aviation, although conditions were still marginal at best – there was now even the odd flurry of snow among the clouds. Jack Lidsey and Sid Quicke got airborne in a BE2f, serial number A3154, on an artillery observation task with the 9th Canadian Siege Battery. A3154 was a brand-new aeroplane (built by Wolseley Motors) that was originally intended as a BE2c but had been fitted with a new design of wing in the factory that gave improvements in speed and rate of climb; the machine had only arrived on No. 16 Squadron's strength a week before. For self-protection, they took with them two Lewis Guns, one alongside Sid's cockpit and the other with Jack in the front, since they were to have no fighter escort. They were detailed to spot for the Canadian guns against targets on Vimy Ridge, and planned to fly parallel to the front line on the British side of it, close to Neuville-Saint-Vaast. Flying the aeroplane would not have been easy for Quicke that day because the gusting easterly wind would have been at ninety degrees to his track as he followed the front line, requiring constant pressure on the controls to keep the BE in a straight line and steady enough for Lidsey to observe, register and correct the fall of shot. Also, to give Jack a clear view of the ground, Sid would have had to have kept the aeroplane below the cloud, which was already low, thereby handing the advantages of cover and altitude to any would-be attacker. Matthew Boddington, owner and pilot of a replica BE2, states that flying the aeroplane in such conditions would have been 'quite a huge effort'.

Reports of British air activity, witnessed from the German trenches, reached La Brayelle during the day, so von Richthofen decided to get into the air and try his luck. Given the weather, he went alone since keeping several aircraft together and in formation amid low cloud and the stiff wind would have proved difficult, if not impossible. Some of his *Jasta* pilots also took off as singletons to hunt for the enemy that afternoon. The messages he had seen said that the British aircraft were operating on their own side of the lines, at around '1,000 metres altitude, in spite of bad weather and a strong east wind'.[178] He had been in the air for an hour when he spotted 'at 800 metres [altitude] a large number of enemy artillery fliers', as expected flying over their own territory; they 'sometimes approached our front, but never passed it'.

During his early days as a pilot, von Richthofen had been taught the art of aerial combat by his mentor Oswald Boelcke, one of the war's earliest fighter aces and often considered the 'father' of air fighting tactics. One of the mantras Boelcke had handed down, as part of the so-called 'Dicta Boelcke' (a set of maxims for air fighting), was 'If you are above the enemy lines, always keep your own retreat in mind.' The Red Baron would almost certainly have had that rule at the forefront of his mind since he would have to fly into the squall on his way back, and the resulting loss of ground speed would have made him vulnerable to British anti-aircraft fire, as well as to anyone in the trenches who fancied his chances with a rifle or machine gun. Also, his fuel consumption rate would have dramatically increased as his Albatros's Mercedes engine fought against the headwind, so he would have needed to keep a constant watch on his fuel gauge, and make mental calculations to make sure he had enough petrol to get home.

Boelcke also made it clear to secure the tactical advantage before attacking; speed, height and position were all vital to bringing down an enemy aircraft successfully. Von Richthofen selected his target from the gaggle that he had seen, and began stalking it – it was Lidsey and Quicke's machine. According to the Red Baron's combat report, he tried 'several vain attempts' to bring down the BE2 before finally, 'half hidden by cloud', he managed to get into a favourable position and take his prey 'by surprise'.

Quicke was flying the BE2 quite low, at less than 2,000 feet (600 metres on the report), almost certainly because of the low cloud base. Mindful of his mentor's teachings, von Richthofen this time closed right in to his quarry before opening fire. The prolonged contest had taken him about one kilometre beyond his own lines, probably about as far over enemy territory as he was comfortable with, given the weather. In total, he sent 500 rounds of 7.92mm ammunition streaking towards the British machine from his twin Spandau machine guns, observing that 'the adversary made the mistake of flying in a straight line when he tried to evade me, and thus he was just a wink too long in my fire'.[179] Rounds from the Albatros's guns struck either the BE2's engine or fuel tanks, or possibly both, since the critically wounded aircraft quickly began to emit black smoke. Von Richthofen watched as 'suddenly, he made two uncontrolled curves and dashed, smoking, to the ground. The plane was completely ruined. It fell in section F.3.'[180] The Red Baron had claimed his twenty-ninth victory.

Lidsey had been sending Morse code corrections to the Canadian gun battery via the artillery observation dugout far below. As soon as the transmissions went dead, the gunner in the dugout ran above ground to see what had gone wrong. It could have meant a failure of the wireless equipment – a far from uncommon occurrence – or something far worse. Through his binoculars, he saw the BE2, caught without an escort, 'striving to defend themselves and escape from a fast enemy scout machine which attacked them repeatedly'.[181] The artillery officer watched as 'the end came in five minutes when the English machine was suddenly enveloped in a cloud of black smoke, and a second later plunged to earth'.[182] With the gruesome scenario played out, he telephoned No. 16 Squadron to report what he had seen and asked for a replacement aircraft to be sent to continue the task.[183] Another witness on the ground, a Captain Briston, reported seeing the BE2 downed by 'a big red enemy plane'.

For Jack Lidsey, there would have been several terrifying seconds as he plummeted towards the earth, trapped in the spiralling, burning aircraft with no means of escape. Parachutes were not then carried in RFC aircraft[184] because the Air Board felt that they were too heavy and cumbersome, with the added weight adversely affecting aircraft with already poor performance, such as the BE2. Unofficially, the board considered that 'the presence of such an apparatus might impair the fighting spirit of pilots and cause them to abandon machines which might otherwise be capable of returning to base for repair'. Many aircrew carried a revolver to give themselves a swift end rather than face being burned alive or waiting to be smashed into the ground.

The stricken BE2 crashed at a geographical feature known as Hill 123, just north of Neuville-Saint-Vaast, at around 5.30 p.m. German time, close to the battery of guns with which it had been working. Canadian medics rushed to the scene, finding Sid Quicke's lifeless body in the rear cockpit, but Jack Lidsey still alive – barely – in the front. It must have been a tricky operation to extract him from the tangled wreckage of A3154 without causing further injury, but they managed to do just that, and get him away to medical aid.

Back at Bruay, there was a degree of confusion about the fates of the BE2's crew. Captain Eric Routh, the CO of No. 16 Squadron's 'A' Flight, wrote in his journal that 'Lidsey and a sergeant pilot [sic] were brought down by the "red hun" today. The sergeant may live but it is rather doubtful as he had rather a bad crash on landing; Lidsey was shot in the air. It was not a good day; low cloud prevented proper protection by [fighter] patrols.'[185] Details of the casualties had obviously been mixed up at some point in the reporting.

No. 42 Casualty Clearing Station (CCS), manned by the Royal Army Medical Corps, was situated at Aubigny-en-Artois, around seven miles to the west of the crash site, and was the closest medical facility with any hope of saving Jack's life. Established in February 1916, No. 42 CCS had seen plenty of patients in its time, although it had not always enjoyed the best of reputations. An inspection on 2 June 1916 by the matron-in-chief of the British Expeditionary Force, Maud McCarthy, stated that the CCS 'is not by any means satisfactory, it is dirty, ill-managed and a lack of interest and management everywhere'.[186] Nine months later, however, things were better, due in no small part to McCarthy's tireless and tenacious efforts to improve the general standard of nursing on the Western Front.

Jack was drifting in and out of consciousness when he was brought in to the clearing station, with his injuries so severe that an operation was impossible; in all probability, he would not have survived the trauma of surgery anyway. All that could be done was for the nurses to make him as comfortable as possible and to watch over him as the hours passed. He clung desperately on to life throughout that evening and into the night until, shortly after 3.00 a.m. on Thursday 22 March 1917, aged just twenty-one, Second Lieutenant William John Lidsey succumbed to his wounds, never knowing that he had been recommended for promotion. The matron of No. 42 CCS, Mrs Rain, sent the following letter to his parents on the day that he died:[187]

> Dear Sir
> Your son Lt [sic] Lidsey 16th Squadron RFC was admitted last night, mortally wounded in the head, both legs and arms. Everything was done to give him ease, and he passed away at 3.15am today. He was too bad for operation; nothing could be done for him. He was partially conscious and tried to give his home address – all he said was 'Oxford' – he soon became quite unconscious.
> I am so truly sorry to send you this sad news
> Yours faithfully
> Mrs Rain, Matron.

Jack's shattered body was later taken by the clearing station's orderlies to the nearby Aubigny civilian cemetery (which had been extended at the start of the war to accommodate military burials, first by the French Army and then by the British) where he was buried by his comrades from

No. 16 Squadron. Ironically, this was the same cemetery where Lidsey had acted as a pall bearer at the funeral of his friend Robert Jack less than a month earlier; their final resting places are just six plots apart. At the head of Lidsey's grave they erected a broad wooden cross, marked in black lettering with the simple details of his rank, name and unit, and the date.

No. 16 Squadron's commanding officer, Major Paul Maltby, immediately wrote his condolences to Jack Lidsey's parents, just as he had done to the relatives of all the other casualties that his squadron had suffered during his tenure. Jack's grieving father replied to Maltby from Hardwick House on 30 March, his notepaper edged in black:[188]

> Dear Sir
> I am writing to ask if you will kindly furnish me with the details that preceded the death of my dear son, Lieut W J Lidsey. The loss of my boy is very hard to bear, and any particulars you can give I shall be most grateful for. I presume his belongings will be forwarded here. Apologising for troubling you, & with many thanks in anticipation.
> Yours faithfully
> Wm Lidsey

Major Maltby responded, prompting a second, less formal, letter from William Lidsey senior on 4 April 1917, similarly bordered in the colour of mourning:[189]

> Dear Mr Maltby
> Very many thanks for your kind and sympathetic letter & also for details of our dear son's death. His kit and belongings I have no doubt will arrive in due course. Your expressions help us to bear our grief, and we are very proud that 'he did his bit' willingly & manfully. It is also a great relief to me to know that you laid him to rest beside some of his brother officers in our own lines & where his burial place will be recorded. We shall be most grateful if you will have his grave photographed and a copy forwarded to me. As soon as possible after the war I shall hope to visit Aubigny. I hope when next you visit England, if it is possible, you will call on me; we are

about 80 miles from Town[190] & should be very pleased to see you.
Again, thanking you for your kindness.
Yours very sincerely
Wm Lidsey

Piecing together the eyewitness accounts of von Richthofen and the
artillery officer on the ground, it is apparent that Lidsey and Quicke fought
hard for their lives. That the Red Baron had to attack them several
times, in a protracted fight of around five minutes, and that he expended
a large amount of ammunition to bring down an unescorted aircraft that
was far inferior to his own, suggests that Sid Quicke was using all his flying
skill to try to escape. Jack would without doubt have been frantically
returning fire with his Lewis Gun as von Richthofen made his repeated
passes.

We will never know for certain why Quicke flew straight and level
during that last attack, but there are two possible explanations. First,
rather than being taken by surprise, he was already dead at the controls,
having been hit during von Richthofen's previous attempt to bring them
down. Routh states that 'Lidsey' – although it was actually Quicke – had
been 'shot in the air', which must have been reported by the medics who
recovered his body at the crash site and therefore saw his wounds.
Apart from transposing the names, Routh's other details of the incident
are correct. The BE2's inherent stability could perhaps then have kept it
flying briefly in a straight line, with no pilot to make it to do otherwise,
until the final, fatal volley of shots destroyed its engine and sent it into
its death dive.

In the second scenario, Sid was still alive but was indeed caught
unawares. Perhaps it was a simple case that he and Lidsey just did not
see the red Albatros due to the cloud cover. Maybe they thought that
von Richthofen had broken off his attack, having been unsuccessful
several times already. Even if they had seen their assailant at the last
moment, there would have been no time to manoeuvre away, and if
Quicke had tried to do so, then the BE2's lack of agility meant that it would
not move as rapidly as his frantic inputs on the controls demanded, hence
staying 'just a wink too long' in von Richthofen's fire. With Sid now
dead from that last attack, the pilotless British machine then went into

its 'uncontrolled curves'.

Quicke's corpse was taken from the crash site back to No. 16 Squadron's aerodrome at Bruay. He was buried in the military extension of the town's communal cemetery where many of his squadron comrades had also been interred. Sadly then, although they flew and fought together that day, in death Jack and Sid were separated.

Conclusion

After the First World War, when the British military cemeteries in France and Belgium were formalised and the wooden crosses that marked the graves were replaced with headstones sculpted from Portland stone, relatives of the fallen were sometimes offered the opportunity to bring the original markers home. The families were responsible for either having them shipped back to Britain or for collecting them in person, and the decision on where to place the crosses was also up to them – a number were given to churches; others to schools; some to museums; and many remained in private homes. Most, however, were not brought home due to the costs and logistics involved and were therefore destroyed near to the cemetery where they had stood, usually by burning. The ashes from the pyres were then scattered over the cemeteries. Of those that were brought home, many have since been lost over the intervening 100 years, either through neglect or through being removed and destroyed in the 1960s by young clergy who sought to 'de-glorify' the First World War. A national project to catalogue all the surviving crosses across the United Kingdom can be found at *www.thereturned.co.uk.*

Jack Lidsey's original wooden grave cross hangs on the wall of the chapel at Magdalen College School, Brackley. At some point the cross has been renovated, since the photograph of it in situ above his grave shows it as plain wood whereas it is now whitewashed, and the lettering has been changed. The whitewash ends several inches above the bottom of the cross, indicating that the paint was probably applied while it was still in the ground at the grave; there is no doubt, though, that it is the same cross. There are three other wooden crosses alongside Lidsey's in the chapel, all Old Brackleians. One belongs to Arthur Stace, who had been in Jack's form at school and was the son of Harry Stace, the owner of the auction firm for whom Jack worked after leaving Magdalen. Arthur was killed in a flying accident in 1919 while serving with the Royal Air Force in Belgium, and his parents later commissioned and paid for the school war memorial that stands on the lawn outside the chapel. Thirty-three old boys of the school were killed during the First World War.

The Commonwealth War Graves Commission (CWGC) headstone now marking Lidsey's grave in Aubigny cemetery is interesting insofar as it has the badge of the Royal Air Force engraved at its top, yet Jack died just over a year before the formation of the RAF so was never a member of it. All Royal Flying Corps headstones are like this, and it appears that the reason is that, since the RAF was in existence by the time the permanent headstones were erected in the 1920s, then all airmen casualties were treated as members of the new Service, regardless of their date of death. The CWGC recognises this anomaly and has said that, as the headstones weather and need replacing, the new ones will bear the RFC badge instead, where appropriate.

Families were able to request that a personal message be engraved on the new headstones when the wooden crosses were replaced, and a charge was levied for an inscription at the rate of 3½d per letter, up to a maximum of £1. There was a public outcry against the charge, since many relatives felt that their fallen had already paid a high enough price with their lives, and many families who had lost their breadwinner simply could not afford the outlay. The charge was eventually scrapped. Jack Lidsey's parents chose to have a quotation from Psalm 21 inscribed at the foot of his headstone:

> HE ASKED LIFE OF THEE
> AND THOU GAVEST HIM A LONG LIFE

A further memorial to Lidsey can be found inside the church of St Mary, the main Banbury church. It takes the form of a marble and mosaic plaque and was almost certainly placed there by his family since his father was the vicar's warden at St Mary's. Interestingly, at the top of the plaque is a stylised set of RFC pilot's 'wings', but Lidsey was of course an observer, not a pilot – he was not entitled to wear the pilot's badge.

Jack's father, William Isaac Richard Lidsey, went on to be prominent in Banbury local politics, and was made mayor of the borough in 1922. He rode to hounds with the Warwickshire Hunt until over seventy years old, and was also a justice of the peace. A local authority housing estate was built in the town in the 1960s, and its streets were named after former mayors; one thoroughfare is called Lidsey Road.

Hardwick House still stands and is now a Grade II* listed building. The house and most of the land are no longer in the hands of the Lidsey family and the estate has shrunk considerably over the years. The M40 motorway cuts a diagonal swathe across the eastern part of the estate, while the Hardwick Business Park (built on the old Alcan site after the factory closed in 2008) and new housing developments have swallowed up much of the old farm.

Magdalen College School, Brackley, continued as a boys' grammar school until 1973, when it combined with the local girls' high school and Brackley Secondary Modern School to become a comprehensive school – today, it has academy status. Of its sister establishments, the one in Oxford continues to flourish, while Magdalen College School in Wainfleet, Lincolnshire, closed in 1933 when its functions were transferred to Skegness Grammar School.

The 1/4 (Oxfordshire) Battalion, The Oxfordshire & Buckinghamshire Light Infantry, remained on the Somme until early August 1917 when it was redeployed to the Ypres Salient in Belgium, where it had started its war more than two years earlier. There, the battalion took part in the muddy, bloody slaughter that was the Battle of Passchendaele. In just one day, on 16 August 1917, it lost 65 men killed and a further 105 wounded, with all bar two company officers becoming casualties. Of the five officers killed that day, two were Second Lieutenant Hamilton Jefferson – with whom Lidsey had travelled from England when rejoining the battalion after commissioning – and Captain Andrew Wotherspoon (of the Cameronians), with whom he had shared a day out in Amiens shortly before joining the RFC.

Another Cameronian officer about whom Jack wrote was Second Lieutenant Robert (Guy) Ramsay, who suffered an epileptic fit while with

Lidsey in Amiens on 27 September 1916. Ramsay returned to his own regiment in November that year, having spent just two months with the
Oxfords. He was invalided out of the Army in 1917 'on medical grounds'
rather than because of wounds, so in all probability his discharge was
due to his epilepsy. He was ordained into the Baptist Church after the
war, a calling he followed for the next fifty years in Scotland and England,
and he also published three books, all theological works. Guy Ramsay
died in 1976, aged eighty.

In December 1917 the Oxfordshires were sent to the Italian front, where
they stayed until the end of the First World War. Little by little the men
were repatriated, and by the end of March 1919, everyone was home. A
civic reception was held for the battalion by the city of Oxford, after
which, just over four and a half years after it was raised, 1/4 (Oxfordshire)
Battalion was disbanded.

The Oxfordshire & Buckinghamshire Light Infantry went on to fight
in all theatres during the Second World War, most famously as part of
6th Airborne Division when D Company of the regiment's 2nd Battalion
captured the vital bridges over the Caen Canal and the River Orne in
Normandy during the early hours of D-Day. After the Second World War,
the regiment saw further action against EOKA terrorists in Cyprus in
1956. The regiment was disbanded on 7 November 1958 when it was
absorbed into the new Green Jackets Brigade, becoming the 1st Battalion,
the Green Jackets. A vestige of the Ox & Bucks remained, though, as they
kept their old Regiment of Foot numbers, 43rd and 52nd, in parenthesis.
Further amalgamations saw the Green Jackets become The Royal Green
Jackets in 1966, and then in 2005 that name was also lost following the
creation of The Rifles, which took in all the remaining light infantry
regiments.

The locations on the Somme where Jack Lidsey fought while serving
with the Oxfordshires have now all reverted to farmland, while
Ploegsteert Wood near Ypres has re-established itself over the past 100
years or so. The Pozières British Cemetery and Memorial was built
directly on top of Sickle Trench where it joined the Albert to Bapaume
Road, and many of the graves within the cemetery are of men of the
Oxfordshires and the other 145 Brigade battalions who died trying to
take Sickle and Skyline Trenches, as well as Point 79. A farm track now

follows the line of Skyline Trench on the ridge overlooking Thiepval. Point 79 is difficult to find since, unhelpfully, there are two different Points 79 marked on the maps within the Oxfordshire Battalion's War Diary, but with careful reading and deduction, the one that Lidsey attacked three times in August 1916 can be found, in the middle of a crop field. On a visit there in September 2018, the author found a live British Mills bomb lying on the surface of the soil, perhaps a relic of the protracted bombing duel that Jack had there with the enemy.

The Arras offensive, the British part of General Robert Nivelle's grand plan for April 1917, was initially a success, but the French Army's failure on the Aisne a week later eventually spelled disaster for the overall strategy. As many had suspected, Nivelle was unable to deliver his much-vaunted forty-eight-hour knockout blow and the attack had largely petered out by the start of May. Rather than Nivelle's hopelessly optimistic prediction of 10,000 casualties, the French Army alone suffered in the region of 187,000 men killed, missing, wounded or captured, leading to a mutiny in the Army and Nivelle being sacked. For their part, the British ultimately lost in the region of 158,000 troops despite light casualties and significant territorial gains in the first two days of the assault. During that early phase, Vimy Ridge was attacked most successfully by the Canadian Corps, falling to them within three days of the start of the battle on 9 April at a cost of around 11,000 casualties. Their victory was due in no small part to meticulous planning, training, and the close cooperation between artillery, infantry and aircraft that had been deemed so vital prior to the offensive. The harsh lessons from the Somme the previous year had been learned and overcome.

According to Lidsey's RFC commanding officer, Major Paul Maltby, No. 16 Squadron lost sixty-three aircrew between February and April 1917 during the build-up to, and subsequent battles of, Vimy Ridge and Arras. No. 16 Squadron was one of the hardest-pressed of all RFC units throughout that period. During March, when Jack Lidsey was killed, the RFC as a whole lost more aircraft and crews in that one month than it had throughout the entire year of 1915 at the height of the 'Fokker Scourge'. April 1917 was so bad for the RFC in terms of attrition that it became known as 'Bloody April'; some 275 British aircraft were destroyed (60 of which were BE2s), with 421 aircrew casualties (of which around half were killed) across the squadrons that were engaged in supporting the Nivelle offensive.[191] The German squadron that scored the highest number of victories against the RFC during that horrific month was, of course, von Richthofen's *Jasta 11*. In a dissertation written while at the RAF Staff College after the war, Maltby observed that: 'It was difficult trying to maintain the morale of the Squadron, and to get the work done, but thanks to the example which the older hands set, both were kept up. The majority of casualties occurred amongst pilots newly out from England and were the result of inexperience combined with inferior aircraft. Once past a certain point, pilots rarely became casualties.[192]'

After the failure of Nivelle's plan, Paul Maltby was sent back to England for a rest in June 1917 where he was ordered to form a new flying training squadron. By that stage of the war, he was, he openly admitted, 'fairly near the end of my tether. The last four months at very high pressure coming on the top of some eighteen months continual flying in France was too much. I dreaded the thought of what would happen, so far as the running of the Squadron was concerned, if the break-through, which we were all hoping for [the Nivelle Offensive], actually materialised. This would have entailed the same amount, or more, [of] work under much more difficult circumstances.'[193]

The outdated BE2s of No. 16 Squadron were eventually replaced by the Royal Aircraft Factory RE8 (nicknamed 'Harry Tate' in rhyming slang after a popular music hall comedian of the time) in May 1917, although the BE2 carried on flying with the RFC, providing service in the communications and liaison roles. The RE8 was no better, and in some respects arguably worse, than the BE2, and enjoyed an equally dismal reputation. Some improvements were incorporated in the RE8's design, such as moving the observer to the rear seat, but like the BE2 it was built to be inherently stable so offered no real enhancement in terms of air combat agility. The RE8 was also more difficult to fly than its predecessor, particularly since it was much heavier and therefore needed a far higher landing speed than former BE2 pilots were used to. Because the aircraft gave almost no warning that it was about to stall, many unwary pilots realised too late that their airspeed was insufficient to remain airborne. The RE8's limitations were highlighted starkly on 13 April 1917 when six of them, all operated by No. 59 Squadron, were shot down within a matter of minutes by *Jasta 11*. However, Major Maltby said that, after his squadron's experiences with the BE2, the new aeroplane was 'more than welcome' and that 'everyone liked them very much'. [194] Whatever the truth, the RE8 was hastily withdrawn from service almost as soon as the war had finished, ironically before the BE2 was itself fully retired.

No. 16 Squadron Royal Flying Corps saw active service for the rest of the First World War, becoming a squadron of the newly created Royal Air Force on 1 April 1918. The squadron disbanded in 1919 but re-formed in 1924, serving throughout the Second World War and then on into the jet age. During the first Gulf War of 1991 when Iraq invaded and occupied Kuwait, the squadron deployed its Panavia Tornado GR1 aircraft to Tabuk in Saudi Arabia, from where it carried out perilous bombing missions against Iraqi airfields and other military targets. Disbanded later the same year, the squadron number plate was passed to No. 226 Operational Conversion Unit, which trained pilots to fly the SEPECAT Jaguar ground-attack/tactical reconnaissance aircraft, becoming No. 16 (Reserve) Squadron. With the imminent withdrawal from service of the Jaguar, the squadron was disbanded once more in 2005 and remained dormant for three years until, in 2008, another training unit, this time No. 1 Elementary Flying Training School, took on the squadron number and its reserve status. No. 16 Squadron continues to fly today, operating the Grob Tutor aircraft from RAF Wittering.

Paul Maltby stayed on in the nascent Royal Air Force after the Armistice, rising steadily through the ranks. By 1942, he had been promoted to air vice marshal and was the air officer commanding Commonwealth air forces in Java (and subsequently commander of all British forces in the region) when Sumatra was overrun by the Japanese. He spent the rest of the Second World War as a prisoner of war, and throughout his incarceration he battled bravely with his captors over the appalling living conditions and treatment of his fellow prisoners. He was awarded a knighthood after the war and was appointed serjeant-at-arms of the House of Lords in 1946, an office he held until 1962. Sir Paul Copeland Maltby died in 1971, aged seventy-eight.

Another of Jack Lidsey's No. 16 Squadron comrades who went on to enjoy a stellar career in the Royal Air Force was Herbert Massey. Despite being badly burnt as a result of being shot down by Werner Voss, he was able to make a return to military flying after the First World War. He went on to command No. 6 Squadron from 1934 to 1937, during which period he saw action with the squadron in the Arab Revolt in Palestine, where he was wounded while flying on operations once again. By the start of the Second World War, Massey had reached the rank of group captain and later commanded RAF Oakington, a bomber station near Cambridge.

Not one to lead from the rear, he occasionally flew on bombing raids over Germany even though it was not his remit to do so. On the night of 2 June 1942, Massey was flying as second pilot in a Short Stirling bomber of No. 7 Squadron during the second so-called 'thousand-bomber raid'. On the way back to Oakington following an attack on Essen, the Stirling was shot down over the Dutch coast south of Vlissingen. The crew managed to bale out successfully and all survived, becoming prisoners of war. Massey, who walked with a limp, was imprisoned at the Stalag Luft III POW camp at Sagan in Poland where, as senior British officer, he authorised the fabled 'Great Escape', which took place from the camp in March 1944. Later that same year, he was repatriated home due to ill health, whereupon Massey was able to report the murder of fifty of the recaptured escapees by the Gestapo as a war crime. In the 1963 film *The Great Escape*, his character (renamed Group Captain Ramsey) was portrayed by the actor James Donald, who played the part using a walking stick in a nod to Massey's disability. Herbert Martin Massey later reached the rank of air commodore, was made a Commander of the British Empire, and was awarded the Distinguished Service Order for his service in Palestine in addition to the Military Cross he had won in the First World War. He was also Mentioned in Despatches three times, including twice during the Second World War. He died in 1976, aged seventy-eight. In 2016, a Blue Plaque was unveiled at Hilton House in Derbyshire to commemorate Massey's birthplace.

Harry Bagot, the pilot of the BE2 shot down by Voss when Lidsey's friend Robert Jack was killed, survived the war and went on to inherit the Bagot baronetcy, becoming the 7th Baron Bagot in 1961 on the death of his cousin. Bagot passed away in 1973, at the age of seventy-nine.

Several fellow aircrew who feature in Jack's diaries were killed after him, either in combat or as a result of flying accidents. Arthur Perryman, whom Lidsey befriended on his way to join the RFC and who joined No. 16 Squadron with him, survived being shot down during 'Bloody April' when, on the 28th, his BE2 was hit in the fuel tank by machine-gun fire from the German trenches while on an early morning artillery observation sortie. He was wounded in the subsequent crash, near Vimy, which wrote off the aircraft being flown by Captain Augustus Bird, who also lived to tell the tale. Perryman recovered and later volunteered for pilot training, for which he was sent to No. 20 Training Squadron based at Harlaxton, near Grantham in Lincolnshire. On 7 January 1918, while on a solo training flight made riskier by mist and snow, his Airco DH6 aircraft was involved in a mid-air collision with another of the squadron's machines, killing both Perryman and the other pilot, a Canadian named Lieutenant William Anderson. Arthur Perryman was twenty-nine years old.

Lieutenant Rodney (Vernon) Franklin, the pilot who took Lidsey for his first-ever flight on 26 November 1916, was killed on 24 June 1917 at the age of twenty. Franklin had been travelling back to France to re-join No. 16 Squadron after three months' sick leave at home in Australia in March 1917, when he was taken off the troop ship in Alexandria and told to stay on in Egypt with No. 58 Training Squadron as an instructor. On the day that he died, he was testing a Martinsyde S.1 fighter when it suffered structural failure and crashed. Vernon Franklin died of his wounds a few hours later.

Second Lieutenant Frederick Gay was just nineteen years old when he died of wounds on 25 March 1917, as a result being shot down the previous day. His observer, Second Lieutenant Arthur Baerlein, was also wounded but survived.

Lieutenant Osbert Knight, having been hit in the arm on 6 March 1917, was badly wounded again, this time in the hand, on 28 March but continued to fly his BE2 for another hour, winning a Military Cross in the process. He was shot down by a German fighter and killed nine days later, on 6 April 1917, along with his observer, Lieutenant U.H. Seguin.

The 22-year-old Captain Arthur Burlton died in a flying accident while with No. 46 Training Squadron at Catterick in Yorkshire, on 30 August 1917, when his BE12 (a single-seat variant of the BE2) collided with a BE2.

The other pilot, one Lieutenant Nelson, was also killed.

Second Lieutenant Charles Crow, aged twenty, was the tenth victim of Manfred von Richthofen's younger brother Lothar, also of *Jasta 11*, who shot Crow down near Vimy on 23 April 1917. Second Lieutenant E. Turner, Crow's observer, was wounded but lived.

Manfred Albrecht Freiherr von Richthofen, the Red Baron, went on to shoot down a confirmed total of 80 Allied aircraft during the First World War (although his actual tally may have been closer to 100), making him the highest-scoring ace of the conflict on all sides. Of those confirmed victories, over twenty-one per cent of them were against BE2s. He was killed on 21 April 1918 close to the village of Vaux-sur-Somme while engaged in a low-level dogfight with Sopwith Camels of No. 209 Squadron, Royal Air Force. Von Richthofen was hit by a single bullet, in all probability fired from the ground (although controversy still rages about who fired the fatal shot), which struck him in the chest. Despite his wound, he managed to get his aeroplane on to the ground, albeit roughly, and then died almost immediately; he was twenty-five years old. As he had come down on the British side of the lines, his famous red-painted Fokker Triplane was raided for souvenirs by the Australian troops in the area. Fragments of the fabric and other parts of the aeroplane can be found in various museums and collections around the world today. Manfred von Richthofen was given a burial with full military honours by the British in the village of Bertangles near Amiens. After the war, his body was exhumed and reinterred in the newly created German military cemetery at Fricourt, on the Somme, before being dug up once more in 1925 and taken back to Germany where he was given a state funeral at the Invalidenfriedhof cemetery in Berlin. This was not to be his final resting place, however. During the Cold War the cemetery lay just inside the Soviet zone, right at the boundary with the British sector, and was occasionally used as an escape route by East Germans fleeing to the West. The large memorial stone over von Richthofen's grave was damaged by bullets fired during attempts to stop the escapees, so in 1975 he was disinterred and moved for the last time to the Richthofen family plot at the Südfriedhof in Wiesbaden.

Of the 'very nice young French lady' from Bruay whom Jack met on the train and 'very much hoped to see again', there was no further mention.

Maps

MAP 1

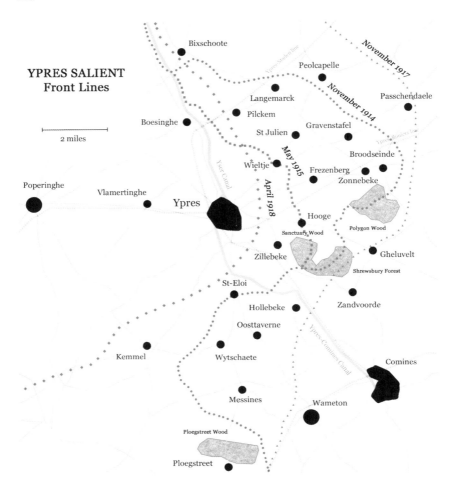

**YPRES SALIENT
Front Lines**

2 miles

The Ypres Salient 1914 – 1918.

MAP 2   169

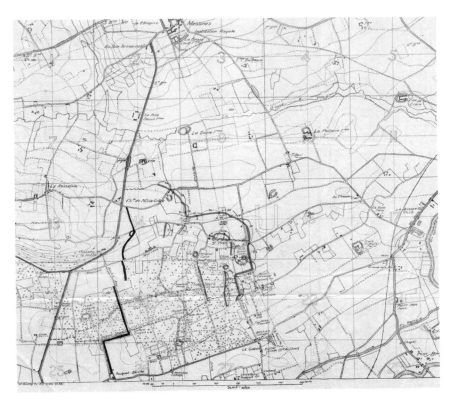

Trench map showing British positions at Ploegsteert Wood, June 1915. *(Crown Copyright)*

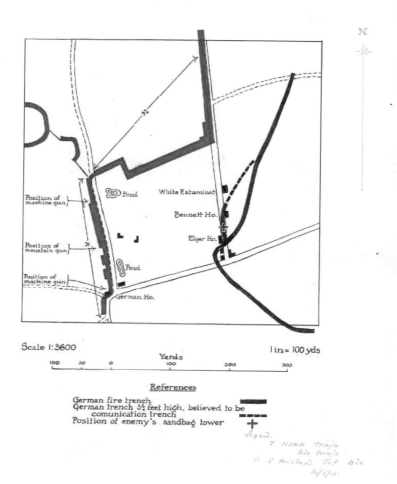

Rough sketch to accompany report on destruction of enemy's
Sandbag Tower

Enlargement of square U.21.b

Scale 1:3600   1 in = 100 yds

Yards

References

German fire trench
German trench 3½ feet high, believed to be
    comunication trench
Position of enemy's sandbag tower

Sketch map showing the location and destruction of the German sandbag observation tower opposite
the Oxfordshire's trenches on 12 May 1915. The 'German fire trench' is the bold line to the right of
the map. *(Crown Copyright)*

MAP 4

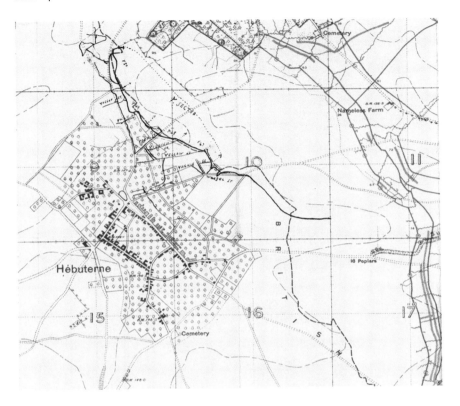

Trench map showing British and German positions at Hébuterne, June 1915. *(Crown Copyright)*

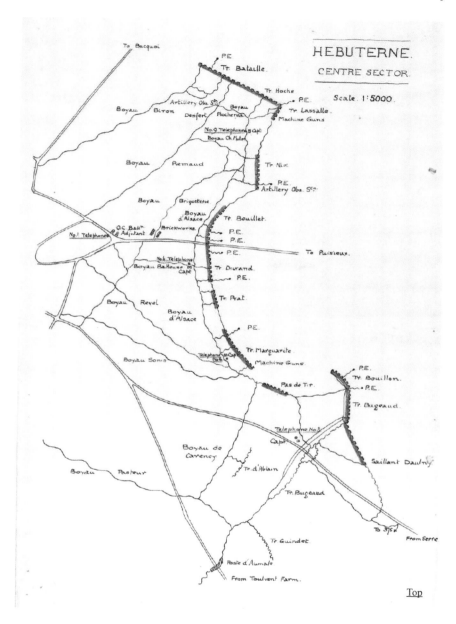

Sketch map of British trenches in the Central (G) Sector at Hébuterne, June 1915. The British have retained the French trench names; note the brickworks just behind the front line in the centre of the map, described by Lidsey as a particularly dangerous location. *(Crown Copyright)*

MAP 6   173

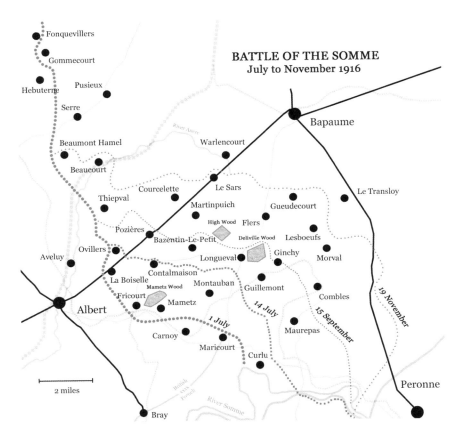

BATTLE OF THE SOMME
July to November 1916

Fonquevillers
Gommecourt
Pusieux
Hebuterne
Serre
Beaumont Hamel
Beaucourt
Thiepval
Courcelette
Warlencourt
Le Sars
Bapaume
Le Transloy
Martinpuich
Gueudecourt
Pozières
High Wood
Flers
Bazentin-Le-Petit
Deliville Wood
Lesboeufs
Ovillers
Aveluy
Longueval
Ginchy
Morval
Contalmaison
La Boiselle
Mametz Wood
Montauban
Guillemont
Combles
Fricourt
Mametz
14 July
15 September
19 November
Albert
1 July
Carnoy
Maurepas
Maricourt
Curlu
Peronne
2 miles
Bray

River Ancre
River Somme
British
French

The Battle of the Somme 1 July – 18 November 1916.

MAP 7

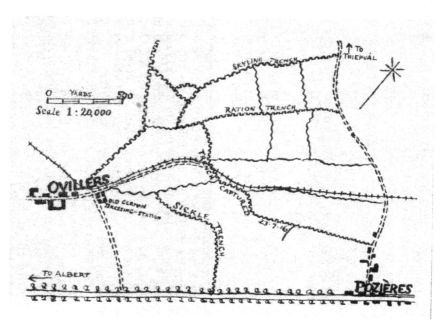

Sketch map showing the relative locations of Sickle, Skyline and Ration trenches, and the trench captured on 23 July 1916 when Lidsey's 3 Platoon was almost wiped out. *(Pickford)*

MAP 8   175

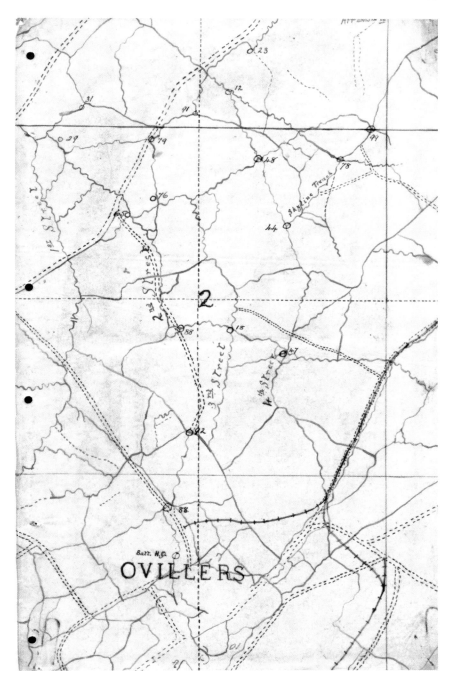

Sketch map showing Skyline Trench (Points 44-78-99 and beyond) with Point 79 to the northwest.
(Crown Copyright)

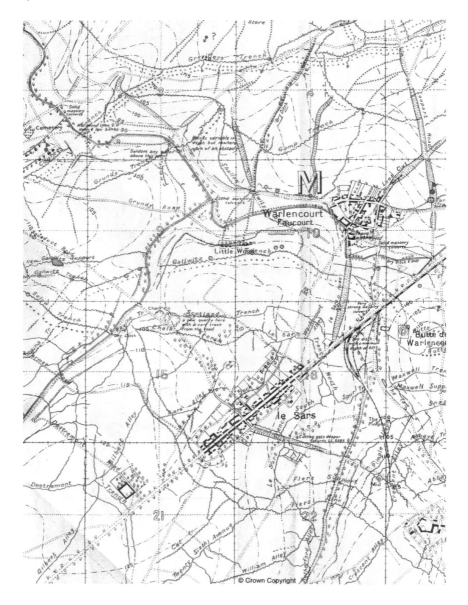

Trench map showing positions around le Sars and the Butte De Warlencourt, October 1916. Chalk Trench is just north of le Sars, with the Butte on the centre-right edge of the map. 26th Avenue Trench is at the bottom centre. *(Crown Copyright)*

MAP 10   177

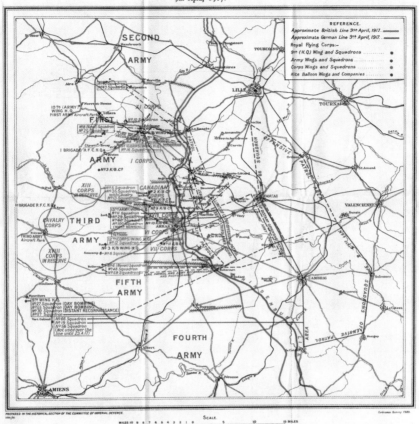

The disposition of Royal Flying Corps squadrons during the build-up to the Arras Offensive, Spring 1917. *(Alamy Stock Photo)*

Acknowledgements

There is an oft-quoted saying that 'we all have a book in us'. While that may be true, books such as this are seldom written in isolation, and depend upon the help of others to bring them to fruition.

My thanks must first go to the Lidsey family, especially Emma, without whose support and trust this book would never have been started. Although Jack Lidsey's diaries are available for the public to view at both the Imperial War Museum and the RAF Museum at Hendon, I wanted to write his story with the approval and input of his family – the 'authorised' version. Having never met me, Emma sent me her treasured copies of the diaries to work from, and she has been on hand throughout the writing of the book to fill in gaps and furnish me with photographs and letters as she has come across them in various family attics.

I would also like to express my gratitude to Steve Brew, aviation history author and friend, who I first approached for guidance when I finally decided to write the book. Steve gave me the encouragement to go ahead and has given me much welcome and valuable guidance since.

The following people, in alphabetical order, have provided me with considerable and generous assistance through their time, advice, material and permissions: **Mark Banning**; **Dr Charlotte Berry**, college archivist at Magdalen College, Oxford; **Barry Blades**; **David Burge** of Shipston-on-Stour & District Local History Society; **Tilly Burn** at

Oxford University Archives; **Alicia Burton**; **Colin Buxton**;
Lauren Carpenter at Northamptonshire Records Office; **Ed Church**;
Flight Lieutenant Rupert Clark, No. 16 Squadron history officer;
Ursula Corcoran at the Soldiers of Oxfordshire Museum;
Edward Crichton at Lacy, Scott & Knight (Auctioneers) of Bury
St Edmunds; **David Davies**, photographer at Stow Maries Great War
Aerodrome, Essex; **Dick Forsythe**, chief trustee of the WW1 Aviation
Heritage Trust; **Norman Franks**; **Derek Gillard**; **Tim Hadfield** of the
Old Brackleians Society; **Barry Hawkins**, Downham Market
auctioneer and land agent; **Dan Hill** at Herts at War; **Richard Knight**;
Brian Little of the Banbury Historical Society; **Andrew North** at
Northamptonshire Records Office; **Kevin Northover**;
Jane Pavia-Davis; **Jason Rush** at Magdalen College School, Brackley;
and **Ben Smith**.

My thanks go to Matthew Boddington and Jean-Michel Munn, both
pilots of replica BE2s, for their insights into flying the aeroplane.
Matthew kindly allowed me to visit and photograph his aeroplane,
based at Sywell airfield, and to sit in the observer's position; it was not
until I had done this that I had an appreciation of what Jack Lidsey
had endured.

For six months during my twenty-six years of service in the RAF,
I had the pleasure of serving on the staff of Lieutenant-General
Jonathon Riley during his tenure as senior British military adviser to
the United States Central Command in Tampa, Florida. General Riley
is a noted military historian and author, and he has given me sage
advice about writing. My sincere thanks go to General Riley for
making time in his busy schedule to kindly write the Foreword for
this book.

Especial thanks to Clare for her support and encouragement during
the writing of this book, and I offer my sincere apologies for all the
times she has tried to talk to me while I was writing and received a
vague, distracted response.

Quotes from documents from the Imperial War Museum,
The National Archives, Hansard, the RAF Museum, Hendon and the
London Gazette that have been reproduced in this book have been

licensed under the terms of the Open Government Licence. The author has sought to establish and acknowledge the copyright holders of all photographs and materials used in this work. Should you become aware of any material that you believe has not been correctly acknowledged, this author welcomes contact via the publisher, and all reasonable endeavours will be made to correct the error. As for any factual inaccuracies, they are entirely mine.

Endnotes

1   *Kelly's Directory of Worcestershire*, 1900.

2   *A History of the County of Gloucester: Volume 6* (London: Victoria County History, 1965).

3   1881 census.

4   Northamptonshire Records Office (NRO): 2003/194/1/2; Magdalen College School, Brackley, Register of Admissions.

5   Cotswold Archaeological Trust.

6   *A History of the County of Oxford: Volume 10, Banbury Hundred* (London: Victoria County History, 1972).

7   Historic England; source ID 1200559.

8   *The Banbury Guardian*: 22 July 2008.

9   Forrester, E.G., *A History of Magdalen College School Brackley, Northamptonshire 1548–1949* (E.N. Hillier & Sons Ltd; Buckingham, 1950), p. 70.

10   Ibid., p. 173.

11   NRO: 2003/194/1/2; Magdalen College School, Brackley, Register of Admissions.

12   1911 census.

13   Forrester, *A History of Magdalen College School Brackley*, p. 2.

14   Ibid., pp. 5–11.

15   The author's brother recalls boys being punished if they were seen playing football in the 1960s.

16   NRO: 2000/236, Box 10: *The Brackleian*, 1884–1923.

17   Ibid.

18   Ibid.

19   Ibid.

20   P.S. Timms won every event in both track and field that year, from the 100 yards to the mile, and the high and long lumps.

21   NRO: 2000/236, Box 10: *The Brackleian*, 1884–1923.

22   Ibid.

23   Forrester, *A History of Magdalen College School Brackley*, p. 114.

24   Ibid.

25   Ibid., p. 177.

26   Ibid., p. 195.

27   The Magdalen Cadet Corps did not form until 1915, and the OTC much later, between the wars.

28   NRO: 2000/236, Box 10: *The Brackleian*, 1884–1923.

29   Ibid.

30   The Acland Report 1911: Report of the Consultative Committee on Examinations in Secondary Schools.

31   NRO: 2003/194/1/2; Magdalen College School, Brackley, Register of Admissions.

32   NRO: 2000/236, Box 10: *The Brackleian*, 1884–1923.

33   Ibid.

34   Ibid.

35   Simkins, Peter, *Kitchener's Army: The Raising of the New Armies, 1914–16* (Barnsley, South Yorkshire: Pen & Sword Military, 2007).

36   Pickford, P. (comp.), *The War Record of the 1/4 Battalion Oxfordshire & Buckinghamshire Light Infantry 1914–1918* (Naval and Military Press (first published 1919)), p. 1.

37   Imperial War Museum (IWM): Documents 4566: Private Papers of Second Lieutenant W.R.H. Brown, MC.

38   Ibid.

39   Pickford, *War Record of the 1/4 Battalion*, p. 1.

40   Ibid.

41   Ibid., p. 2.

42   IWM: Documents 4566: Private Papers of Second Lieutenant W.R.H. Brown MC.

43   Pickford, *War Record of the 1/4 Battalion*, p. 2.

44   Ibid.

45   Pickford, *War Record of the 1/4 Battalion*, p. 3.

46   'In fortification, a small work, usually a timber stockade, about 6 feet high and loop-holed'; Farrow Edward, S., *A Dictionary of Military Terms* (revised edition 1918), p. 605.

47   British nickname for the German 15cm artillery shell.

48   Lidsey was in fact in Belgium.

49   The National Archives (TNA): WO-95-2764-1: 1/4 Battalion Oxfordshire & Buckinghamshire Light Infantry War Diary.

50   Pickford, *War Record of the 1/4 Battalion*, p. 5.

51   Hand grenades, rather than air-dropped munitions.

52   The attack was nowhere near Lille; it was close to Lens.

53   Alec Ruddle died of his wounds the next day.

54   34-year-old Private A. Timms's body was subsequently recovered.

55   TNA: WO-95-2764-1: 1/4 Battalion Oxfordshire & Buckinghamshire Light Infantry War Diary.

56   There is no record of a casualty of this name on this day, although the battalion War Diary does confirm that one man was killed while on patrol.

57   Pickford, *War Record of the 1/4 Battalion*, p. 11.

58   Soldiers' slang for lice or lice-bites.

59   Logs laid across a road, track or trench floor to provide a solid base.

60   TNA: WO-95-2764-1: 1/4 Battalion Oxfordshire & Buckinghamshire Light Infantry War Diary.

61   Pocket watch.

62   Horse-drawn 'general service' wagon.

63   Distinguished Conduct Medal.

64   Pickford, *War Record of the 1/4 Battalion*, p. 12.

65   Root, Laura, *Temporary Gentlemen on the Western Front: Class Consciousness and the British Army Officer, 1914–1918* (University of North Florida, 2006).

66   Lewis-Stempel, John, *Six Weeks; the Short and Gallant Life of the British Officer in the First*

World War (London: Orion, 2011), p. 171.

67 Cloete, Stuart, *A Victorian Son: An Autobiography 1897–1922* (London: Collins, 1972), pp. 266–67.

68 Simpson, Keith, 'The Officers', in *A Nation in Arms: A Social Study of the British Army in the First World War* (Manchester: Manchester University Press, 1985).

69 Holmes, Richard, *Soldiers; Army Lives and Loyalties From Redcoats to Dusty Warriors* (London: HarperPress, 2011), p. 199.

70 The *Copenhagen* was a passenger steamer owned by the Great Eastern Railway. She was torpedoed and sunk by a U-boat in the North Sea on 5 March 1917 with the loss of six lives.

71 Explosive charges contained in metal tubes, which are pushed under barbed wire.

72 British Official History, Military Operations, France & Flanders 1916, Volume 1.

73 A five-second penalty was added for every man arriving over the finishing line 'improperly dressed'.

74 A one-yard start was given for every year of service over two years.

75 TNA: WO-95-2764-1: 1/4 Battalion Oxfordshire & Buckinghamshire Light Infantry War Diary.

76 Ibid.

77 Pickford, *War Record of the 1/4 Battalion*, p. 15.

78 German trench mortars.

79 TNA: WO-95-2764-1: 1/4 Battalion Oxfordshire & Buckinghamshire Light Infantry War Diary.

80 Ibid.

81 Ibid.

82 Second Lieutenant William Trimmer, aged nineteen.

83 TNA: WO-95-2764-1: 1/4 Battalion Oxfordshire & Buckinghamshire Light Infantry War Diary.

84 Ibid.

85 TNA: WO-95-2764-1: 1/4 Battalion Oxfordshire & Buckinghamshire Light Infantry War Diary.

86 Ibid.

87 He later went on to be promoted to captain and was awarded the OBE.

88 TNA: WO-95-2764-1: 1/4 Battalion Oxfordshire & Buckinghamshire Light Infantry War Diary.

89 IWM: Documents 22595: Private Papers of Captain C.E.R. Sherrington, OBE, MC, 'A Vignette of the Somme – August 1916'.

90 TNA: WO-95-2764-1: 1/4 Battalion Oxfordshire & Buckinghamshire Light Infantry War Diary.

91 Presumably meaning 'unsupported'.

92 Almost killed.

93 TNA: WO-95-2764-1: 1/4 Battalion Oxfordshire & Buckinghamshire Light Infantry War Diary.

94 Ibid.

95 5th Guard Regiment of Foot, nicknamed 'The White Devils'.

96 Royal Engineers.

97 A spiced, currant-filled, flat pastry cake similar to an Eccles cake, traditionally made in Banbury.

98 Forrester, *A History of Magdalen College School Brackley*, p. 202.

99 Fortescue had been wounded in the first attack on Sickle Trench back in July, and had been hospitalised in Rouen since then.

100 Possibly tank D18, commanded by Lieutenant Enoch.

101 Pickford, *War Record of the 1/4 Battalion*, p. 23.

102 DLI Museum & Arts Centre, Durham.

103 Royal Army Medical Corps.

104 Twenty-year-old Lieutenant Charles Barton was listed as missing on 7 April 1917; his body was never recovered.

105 Pickford, *War Record of the 1/4 Battalion*, p. 24.

106 Ibid.

107 TNA: AIR 1/754/204/4/77: Establishment of RFC Wireless School at Brooklands.

108 TNA: AIR 1/1164/204/5/2546: Notes for Future Observers Training Manual.

109 Ibid.

110 TNA: AIR 1/997/204/5/1241: Training of Pilots and Observers.

111 Ibid.

112 TNA: AIR 1/2405/303/4/5: Final report of the Committee on the Administration and Command of the RFC.

113 TNA: AIR 1/2148/209/3/199: Training in France: Observer Courses.

114 TNA: AIR 1/2389/228/11/98: An Account by Students of War Experiences: Wg Cdr P.C. Maltby.

115 Lewis, Cecil. *Sagittarius Rising* (Penguin Books, 1983; first published by Peter David Ltd, 1936), p. 51.

116 Ibid., p. 52.

117 IWM: Documents 20671: Private Papers of Wing Commander E.J.D. Routh.

118 Hansard; House of Commons Air Service Debate, 17 May 1916, Volume 82, cc1545-72.

119 Ibid.

120 Introduced in mid-1916 for aircraft; prior to that, the RFC used the standard infantry forty-seven-round magazine.

121 TNA: AIR 1/1164/204/5/2546: Notes for Future Observers Training Manual.

122 IWM: Documents 20671: Private Papers of Wing Commander E.J.D Routh.

123 TNA: AIR 1/2389/228/11/98: An Account by Students of War Experiences: Wg Cdr P.C. Maltby.

124 Ibid.

125 British single-seat 'pusher'-type fighters also built by the Royal Aircraft Factory.

126 A trailing wireless aerial on a spool had to be unwound from the BE2 when transmitting, and then wound back in again once the task was finished.

127 TNA: AIR 1/1219/204/5/2634/50: Air Combat Reports: 16 Squadron, RFC, October–December 1916.

128 *Jasta* was a contraction of the German word *Jagdstaffel*, meaning 'fighter squadron'.

129 Coincidentally, Mulholland became the CO of No. 16 Squadron in 1928.

130 Benbow was the only 'ace' of the war on the FE8, claiming a total of eight victories on the type before being shot down and killed on 30 May 1918 while flying an SE5a fighter.

131 Sergeant first class.

132 Cole, Christopher (ed.), *Royal Flying Corps Communiques 1915–1916* (London: Tom Donovan Publishing Ltd, 1990), p. 326.

133 IWM: Documents 20671: Private Papers of Wing Commander E.J.D Routh.

134 Counter-battery patrols involved spotting the muzzle flashes of German artillery, and then directing British fire back against them.

135 Cole, RFC *Communiques* 1915–1916, pp., 328–29.

136 Glass negative photographic plates.

137 Nickname for a French soldier; freely translated as 'hairy one'.

138   This consisted of keeping in close touch with, and reporting the position of, troops in the front line during active operations.

139   TNA: AIR1/1356/204/19/67 A and B: 16 Squadron, RFC, Miscellaneous Correspondence.

140   There is no record of the loss of an FE2b on this day. The FE8 was most likely to have been that from No. 40 Squadron, shot down by Manfred von Richthofen near Lens.

141   TNA: AIR 1/686/21/13/2250: Combat Reports of Captain Baron von Richthofen.

142   Franks, Norman, Giblin, Hal and McCrery, Nigel, *Under the Guns of the Red Baron* (London: Grub Street, 2000), pp. 59–60.

143   Oswald Boelcke, the squadron commander.

144   von Richthofen, Manfred, *Der Rote Kampfflieger* (1917).

145   Ibid.

146   TNA: AIR 1/2389/228/11/98: An Account by Students of War Experiences: Wg Cdr P.C. Maltby.

147   Lidsey states an Albatros in his diary, but a Roland in his log book; it was probably the former – misidentification was a very common occurrence on both sides.

148   TNA: AIR 1/1411/204/28/42: 40 Squadron, RFC: Combat in the Air Reports, 1 September 1916–31 May 1917.

149   TNA: AIR 1/1219/204/5/2634/49: Combats in the Air: 16 Squadron, RFC, January 1917–February 1917.

150   Ibid.

151   Crewed by Lieutenants F. Brown and H. Fowler.

152   Possibly Second Lieutenant L. Carter of No. 29 Squadron, who was flying an Airco DH2.

153   Dropping artillery shells just in front of attacking troops, and 'walking' the barrage forward as the infantry advanced.

154   TNA: AIR 1/2389/228/11/98: An Account by Students of War Experiences: Wg Cdr P.C. Maltby.

155   They put the wrong date on the report – 4 February rather than 4 March.

156   TNA: AIR 1/1219/204/5/2634/48: Combats in the Air: 16 Squadron RFC March 1917

157   TNA: AIR 1/1354/204/19/67 A and B: 16 Squadron RFC Miscellaneous Correspondence

158   TNA: AIR 1/2116/207/57 Communiques July 1915 – November 1918

159   TNA: AIR 1/1219/204/5/2634/48: Combats in the Air: 16 Squadron, RFC, March 1917.

160   von Richthofen, *Der Rote Kampfflieger*.

161   TNA: AIR 1/686/21/13/2250: Combat Reports of Captain Baron von Richthofen.

162   Franks, Giblin and McCrery, *Under the Guns of the Red Baron*, p. 73.

163   This was probably true – Gosset-Bibby had been hit in the head by von Richthofen's bullets before crashing.

164   TNA: AIR 1/1354/204/19/57: 16 Squadron, RFC, Officer Casualties.

165   Franks, Giblin and McCrery, *Under the Guns of the Red Baron*, p. 73.

166   Routh himself was not infallible, though – he was shot down and wounded on 21 April 1917 by Kurt Wolff.

167   IWM: Documents 20671: Private Papers of Wing Commander E.J.D. Routh.

168   TNA: AIR 1/1219/204/5/2634/48: Combats in the Air: 16 Squadron, RFC, March 1917.

169   Ibid.

170   TNA: AIR 1/1135/204/5/2224: Correspondence between Air Board and GHQ France: Training of Pilots and Observers.

171   Ibid.

172   TNA: AIR 1/2389/228/11/98: An Account by Students of War Experiences: Wg Cdr P.C. Maltby.

173   TNA: AIR 1/686/21/13/2250: Combat Reports of Captain Baron von Richthofen.

174 Franks, Giblin and McCrery, *Under the Guns of the Red Baron*, p. 81.

175 TNA: AIR 1/1354/204/19/57: 16 Squadron, RFC, Officer Casualties.

176 Franks, Giblin and McCrery, *Under the Guns of the Red Baron*, p. 81.

177 Probably the Bristol F2a fighter; its introduction into service was timed to coincide with the Arras offensive.

178 TNA: AIR 1/686/21/13/2250: Combat Reports of Captain Baron von Richthofen.

179 Ibid.

180 Ibid.

181 Gibbons, Floyd, *The Red Knight of Germany* (London: Cassell & Company, 1967; first published 1927), p. 156.

182 Ibid.

183 Gibbons states in his book that this was Lidsey and Quicke's second sortie of the day, but no records of an earlier flight exist; given the weather that day, it is unlikely that they had flown previously.

184 Although they were issued to observation balloon crews.

185 IWM Documents 20671: Private Papers of Wing Commander E.J.D. Routh.

186 TNA: WO95/3989/3: Headquarters Branches and Services. Matron in Chief, May–June 1916.

187 Collection of the RAF Museum, Hendon.

188 TNA: AIR/1/1354/204/19/57: 16 Squadron, RFC, Officer Casualties.

189 Ibid.

190 London.

191 Bechtold, Mike, 'Bloody April Revisited: The Royal Flying Corps at the Battle of Arras 1917', in *British Journal for Military History, Volume 4, Issue 2, February 2018*, p. 50.

192 TNA: AIR 1/2389/228/11/98: An Account by Students of War Experiences: Wg Cdr P.C. Maltby.

193 Ibid.

194 Ibid.

Index

SHIPS